D1163491

The Death of Franz Liszt

Based on the Unpublished Diary

of His Pupil Lina Schmalhausen

Franz Liszt, oil portrait by Mihály Munkácsy (1886).

THE DEATH OF
Franz Liszt

Based on the Unpublished Diary
of His Pupil LINA SCHMALHAUSEN

Introduced, Annotated, and Edited
by ALAN WALKER

Cornell University Press

Ithaca and London

First published 2002 by Cornell University Press

Printed in the United States of America

Library of Congress Cataloging-in-Publication Data

Schmalhausen, Lina 1864–1928.
    [Liszts Letzte Lebenstage. English]
The death of Franz Liszt : based on the unpublished diary of his pupil Lina Schmalhausen / introduced, annotated, and edited by Alan Walker.
    p. cm.
Translation of "Liszts Letzte Lebenstage" by L. Schmalhausen.
Includes bibliographical references (p.) and index.
  ISBN 0-8014-4076-9 (cloth : alk. paper)
  1. Schmalhausen, Lina, 1864–1928—Diaries. 2. Pianists—Germany—Diaries. 3. Liszt, Franz, 1811–1866—Death and burial. I. Walker, Alan, 1930– II. Title.
  ML417.S295 A3 2002
  780′.92—dc21   2002005791

Contents

Illustrations

Preface

I first came across the unpublished diary of Lina Schmal-hausen in 1977 during a research trip to Weimar. In those days I was heavily engaged in the writing of the first volume of my life of Liszt, *The Virtuoso Years,* and the reason for my visit to the Goethe- und Schiller-Archiv was to collect information about the composer's early career and in particular about his halcyon, life-enhancing years as a touring virtuoso. A detailed account of his death seemed far removed from my immediate interests. Nonetheless, I became curious about the document and asked to inspect it because none of the biographies with which I was familiar even mentioned it. The importance of the diary soon became clear to me, as did the reasons for the embargo on its publication, and I spent a good part of that visit to Weimar persuading the head of the archive to allow me to copy this eighty-four page document. The mere presence of the word "embargo" attached to the file created problems that were only resolved with difficulty.

For the next fifteen years the narrative remained among my research papers; that is a very long time, but it allowed me to become familiar with many details of this remarkable document that I might otherwise have overlooked. As I approached the task of writing the final volume of my biography, the problem of how to treat Schmalhausen's painful account of Liszt's last days in Bayreuth loomed large. The document contains many details of an intimate nature hitherto unknown to Liszt scholars. My initial response to them had ranged from mild scepticism to outright disbelief. In the end, however, Schmalhausen's diary became one of the foundations of the chapter "The Death of Liszt" in *The Final Years,* the third volume of my biography, for reasons that I explain in the prologue to that book. The interest aroused by that chapter, which conflicts in a dramatic way with the received narrative that has done duty for an account of Liszt's death for more than a hundred years, brought me to the conclusion that the publication of the entire diary was a necessary next step.

Lina Schmalhausen's German prose is somewhat opaque, and it is written in an untidy Gothic calligraphy. Moreover, the diary shows signs of having been composed in haste, in telegraphic style, and shortly after the events it describes. Since the script contains few, if any, corrections, it may actually be a cleaner version of an earlier draft that no longer exists. I owe a debt to gratitude to Richard Sikora who prepared a preliminary English translation of the text for me to use as a working version. From that beginning, I myself took on the responsibility of rendering Schmalhausen's language into polished English, even where that meant changing some of her sentence structures—either because the originals were repetitive or convoluted, or both. A literal, word-for-word translation of her diary (which was never intended for publication, but rather was planned as an aide-mémoire for Lina Ramann, Liszt's biographer, about whom I shall have more to say in the prologue) would have been hard on the reader and ultimately pointless. I have also provided many annotations in an attempt to bring back to life the various characters depicted in the diary, some of whom have meanwhile fallen into obscurity.

The prologue that follows makes clear the importance of Schmalhausen's diary for Liszt scholars, places it in its proper historical and biographical setting, and provides some information about Schmalhausen herself that is not generally available. It is not often that one has the chance of presenting material that makes a major difference to our understanding of Liszt's life and work, particularly at the threshold of the twenty-first century after so much important research has already been accomplished. The Schmalhausen diary falls into just such a category, however. Her account of Liszt's last ten days in Bayreuth is riveting, and I am privileged to present it to the general reader here.

ALAN WALKER

Acknowledgments

I should like to express my thanks to the Stiftung Weimarer Klassik and the Goethe- und Schiller-Archiv in Weimar, Germany, for permission to publish the Schmalhausen diary in full, in an English translation, and for allowing the photographic reproduction of several pages of the original document; to Frau Evelyn Liepsch, chief music archivist of the Goethe- und Schiller-Archiv, for dealing with various inquiries, in particular those concerning some peripheral correspondence surrounding the origins of the diary and its acquisition by the archive; to Pauline Pocknell and László Jámbor, who read the finished typescript and made a number of valuable suggestions; and to Philip Wults, who provided some irreplaceable insights into the problems of the Bayreuth Festival of 1886 in particular, and of the Wagner family in general.

Liszt and Lina Schmalhausen, Budapest, 1885. Photograph by Károly Koller.

The Death of Franz Liszt

Based on the Unpublished Diary

of His Pupil Lina Schmalhausen

Prologue
The Background

I

Shortly after Liszt's death in Bayreuth, which occurred toward midnight on July 31, 1886, his biographer Lina Ramann contacted Lina Schmalhausen and asked her to provide an account of the last few days of the master's life. Ramann was in the middle of writing the second volume of her authorized life of Liszt, and she knew that a first-hand description of Liszt's illness, his death, and his funeral in the city of Richard and Cosima Wagner would eventually be required for her work, and that it must be captured before memory faded and fiction started to take the place of fact. Ramann herself would have attended the funeral and picked up this information directly; but she was ill and unable to travel, which is how she came to ask Lina Schmalhausen to take on this task instead. Schmalhausen, after all, had been Liszt's pupil for seven years, and had served as his secretary, housekeeper, and caregiver. No one was in a better position, Ramann must have argued, to give her a reliable account of Liszt's farewell to the world.

Ramann had no inkling of the harrowing events that had

occurred in Bayreuth, or that Lina Schmalhausen would capture them so vividly for posterity. Liszt had never intended to visit Bayreuth during that fatal summer of 1886. He had changed his mind at the special urging of his daughter Cosima, who required her father's presence there to drum up support for the flagging Wagner Festival. When Ramann finally read Schmalhausen's account of Liszt's death, which occurred right in the middle of the festival, she knew that she would be unable to use it. Not only did it run counter to the sanitized reports of Liszt's death that had already been put into general circulation by Bayreuth's publicity machine, but also it contained a great deal of personal criticism against those within Liszt's inner circle, and in particular against Cosima Wagner. Ramann concluded that discretion was the better part of valor: Schmalhausen's narrative would have to be shelved. The manuscript had actually been given to Ramann on condition that it be destroyed after she had read it. But Ramann was too cautious a scholar to be bound by such an undertaking. The document eventually found its way into the Goethe- und Schiller-Archiv in Weimar, together with the rest of Ramann's personal papers, and was placed under an embargo, not to be lifted until fifteen years after her death, which occurred in 1912. These instructions were honored, and the embargo was not removed until 1927. Until now, the diary complete has remained unpublished.[1]

No one who is remotely interested in the life and work of Franz Liszt can remain unaffected by Schmalhausen's "Liszts

1. The Schmalhausen diary attracted little attention, and the reasons are not hard to find. By the time the embargo had been removed in 1927, schol-

Letzte Lebenstage." The story it has to tell is one of neglect, family indifference, and medical malpractice. It is a serious indictment against those who were in a position to ease the composer's last moments. Moreover, it makes for sensational biography. It radically alters the way in which we have traditionally been led to view Liszt's death—as a painless departure from this life, his dutiful daughter Cosima at his side, his last word being "Tristan." Such an account was always suspect. We now know it to be absurd; yet it served as the script for the final pages of Liszt's biography for more than a hundred years.[2]

arly interest in Liszt was at a low ebb. At the beginning of World War II, all the papers and manuscripts connected with Liszt, including Ramann's archives, were transferred to the Liszt Museum, known as the Hofgärtnerei, where they were unavailable for research. (The Hofgärtnerei was Liszt's home which later became the museum. It kept the name.) It was not until 1954 that the collection was returned to the Goethe- und Schiller-Archiv, where it became a part of the newly founded Nationale Forschungs- und Gedenkstätten der klassischen deutschen Literatur. The diary is today cataloged under the call number "Ramann's Liszt Bibliothek: GSA 59/362."

Schmalhausen's private letters to Lina Ramann cast more light on this matter (GSA 59/332). See especially her letter dated February 10, 1887, which she evidently wrote at the time that she dispatched the final version of "Liszts Letzte Lebenstage" to Ramann, and which helps us to fix the period during which the diary was written.

2. We find this canard about Liszt dying with the word "Tristan" on his lips coming from biographers as diverse as August Göllerich (GL, p. 189), Julius Kapp (KFL, p. 547), and Sacheverell Sitwell (SL, p. 355). William Wallace even determined that the word was uttered at precisely 10:30 P.M. on the evening of July 31, 1886 (WLWP, p. 181), while conveniently failing to tell his readers how he could possibly have arrived at such a remarkable conclusion. At that point, Liszt had been in a coma for more than twenty hours and had spoken to no one.

II

The first question we have to ask ourselves is: Who was Lina Schmalhausen? Born in Berlin, in 1864, the daughter of a titled landowner, Lina spent an itinerant childhood in Upper Silesia, and then moved with her parents to France. She began her first serious music studies in 1872, in Breslau. Three years later, she was already sufficiently advanced to join Theodor Kullak's piano classes in Berlin. Fortune smiled on her when she substituted "with extraordinary success" (as she herself later put it) for an indisposed pianist scheduled to play at a soirée given at Prince Radziwill's. The Kaiser was present, and he was so impressed with the young girl that he took over the cost of her training so that she could devote all her time to music. Thereafter, Lina played regularly at court concerts. She was not yet fifteen years old.[3]

In the summer of 1879, Lina traveled down to Weimar bearing a letter of introduction to Liszt. It soon became apparent that her piano playing left something to be desired. Whatever success she had enjoyed under the special patronage of the Berlin court did not help her in the most famous masterclasses in the world. Indeed, the literature contains a substantial body of anecdotal evidence to suggest that there were times when she was musically incompetent, and we

3. Practically everything we know about Schmalhausen's early life was related by Lina herself to Anna Morsch, the editor of *Deutschlands Tonkünstlerinnen,* Berlin 1894 (MSD, pp. 172–73). Schmalhausen's high opinion of her own musical talents was not confirmed by independent observations, so we have to move with caution over a difficult stretch of territory.

would do well to review it before proceeding. There had been a disastrous performance of Liszt's A major Concerto at the festival of the *Allgemeiner Deutscher Musikverein,* held in Karlsruhe in May 1885, under the direction of Felix Mottl. At the rehearsal, Schmalhausen apparently could not keep time with the orchestra. The performance only went ahead out of deference to Liszt's wishes. Mottl finally resolved the dilemma by playing the accompaniment on a second piano. Malevolent tongues whispered that Mottl had drowned out her playing whenever it became intolerable.[4] Earlier she had tried out the concerto with August Stradal at the second piano, who reported that it was impossible to accompany her because she played "without rhythm and skipped many measures."[5] As early as the summer of 1881, she had had a confrontation with Hans von Bülow, who had taken over the Weimar masterclass while Liszt was indisposed. Once again it was Lina's rhythmic instability that was her downfall and drew Bülow's ire. "I have heard it said that there are people who

4. NZfM, May 15, 1885, p. 224.

5. SE, p. 102. An account of the concert appeared in AMZ June 1884, issue no. 24, p. 218. Written by the editor Otto Lessmann, the article refers specifically to the triumph enjoyed by Mottl, who, as everybody knew, was caught between a potentially disastrous performance by Schmalhausen on the one hand, and Liszt's insistence that only Schmalhausen would be permitted to play the work on the other. In order to avoid a public scandal, Mottl went to a second piano, and his impromptu accompaniment became the "emergency exit" (*Nothtüre*) as Lessman put it, through which he escaped the dilemma. Arthur Friedheim quarreled with Liszt over his teacher's stubbornness in refusing to back down over his choice of Schmalhausen, and Friedheim adds some color to the story in his memoirs, without disclosing the identity of "the incompetent young woman" (FLL, pp. 163–64).

cannot count to three," Bülow cried scornfully. "But you cannot count *to two*."[6] Lina picked up her music and fled, but the next day Liszt called on her at her residence, apologized to her, and brought her back into the class.[7]

By 1884, feelings against Lina were running high. The other students resented the fact that she had such ready access to Liszt. Their feathers were ruffled, too, when Lina picked up gossip from the group that she then passed on to Liszt. She was nicknamed "Miss Telltale" for this charming activity. Her nemesis was Dori Petersen, a twenty-four-year-old student who was inflamed by jealousy toward Lina and began a whispering campaign against her. When Pauline Apel reported the disappearance of small sums of money from Liszt's desk in the spring of 1884, Dori saw her opportunity. She went to Liszt and pointed the finger of guilt in the only direction that made sense to her. This had the opposite effect of the one intended. Liszt was angered by such innuendos, and Dori was severely chastised.[8] The matter might have ended there had

6. LL, p. 20.

7. These well-documented stories conflict with Lina's own account of her early career, as related to Anna Morsch (MSD, pp. 172–73). There she draws attention to favorable press notices, one of which informs us that Schmalhausen was "a phenomenal master of her instrument," and that she played the works of Liszt with "passion, sensitive execution, and virtuosic technical mastery" (MSD, p. 173).

8. An unpublished run of letters from Liszt to both pupils is preserved in the Goethe- und Schiller-Archiv (Ramann Bibliothek, GSA, 380/3). In his strongly worded reprimand to Dori Petersen, Liszt wrote: "Following your recent behavior toward the Schmalhausen family, you will understand that I cannot receive you now or in the future. The whole intrigue was stirred up by you in a mean-spirited way, and was unfortunately continued."

not Lina brought about her own downfall. That same year she was accused of shoplifting by a Weimar haberdasher. Evidently she had put some lace into her handbag and had walked out of the shop without paying for it. Charges were laid, and Liszt was obliged to intercede. With the help of his good friend Hofrat Carl Gille, the chief magistrate in nearby Jena, he managed to have the charges quashed. Much damage was done, nevertheless, and Lina's reputation was tainted. But the matter did not end there. The indefatigable Dori, who would not be silenced, went to the shopkeeper and had him sign a statement that Lina was indeed guilty as charged, however much Liszt defended her, and she flourished the incriminating document before the class. This so infuriated Liszt that he wrote to Petersen banishing her from the Hofgärtnerei and forbidding her to return to the group until she had delivered an apology. Such a banishment could have jeopardized Petersen's career, so she complied. The witty Xaver Scharwenka, who also attended the class at this time, condensed the clouds of gossip swirling around the affair and distilled them into some clever wordplay:

> Andern etwas wegzusammen
>> In der Kunst recht schmal zu hausen
> Ohn' Begriff von Noten, Pausen
>> Nur zu Klimpern—oh, welch Grausen!
> [To pilfer from others
>> To rummage shallowly in Art
> Without an inkling of notes or rests.
>> Merely tinkling—oh, what horror!][9]

9. Scharwenka's lines kill two birds with one stone. Not only does he play

For the last two years of Liszt's life, the masterclasses were abuzz with this scandal, and if the students had been questioned on the matter they would have replied with one voice that as far as they were concerned Lina was persona non grata. It is a fact that she never attended the Weimar masterclasses again but tried to escape embarrassment by pursuing her studies with Liszt in Rome and Budapest instead. Liszt even helped her to find a teaching appointment in Budapest, and for a time she was on the faculty of a local music school there (the Budai Ének- és Zeneakadémia). Liszt visited her class on March 8, 1886.

While Julius Kapp was preparing his well-regarded biography of Liszt (Berlin, 1909) he evidently raised with Schmalhausen this difficult matter of the theft of money. She provided him with a letter from the composer which included a statement virtually clearing her of blame. She also appears to have ingratiated herself into Kapp's narrative, which adroitly shifts the accusation of theft to an anonymous *male* purloiner.[10] Kapp was still only twenty-six years old

with Lina's name ("schmal zu hausen"—to rummage around), but he also refers to her notorious inability to keep time ("Ohn' Begriff von Noten, Pausen"). I have dealt with the long-standing rivalry between Lina Schmalhausen and Dori Petersen in somewhat greater detail in my life of Liszt, WFL, vol. 3, pp. 412–14.

10. Kapp describes the thief simply as "Herr X—one of Liszt's oldest friends" (KFL, p. 525). From this fatal statement it was a simple matter to place Dr. Carl Gille in the dock, that same magistrate who had helped to quash charges of theft brought earlier against Lina herself. Did he not have free access to the Hofgärtnerei? Did he not possess a duplicate key to Liszt's desk? Was he not "one of Liszt's oldest friends?" From this flimsy chain of evidence Gille should have had no difficulty in escaping. But Kapp's biog-

when he published his biography of Liszt, and Schmalhausen's testimony evidently made an impression on him. When Carl Lachmund (an American pupil who was attending the masterclass at the same time as Schmalhausen) read these pages, he was so incensed that he made a retrospective addition to the diary he had kept during the Weimar years, which points the finger of guilt once more in Schmalhausen's direction by making it plain that it was Lina's hand which was caught in the desk drawer.[11]

Did news of Lina's brush with the law reach Cosima's ears? It would go far to explain her distrust of the young woman and her refusal to have her in the house during Liszt's final days. It would also explain why Liszt, having given Lina the precious autograph of his oratorio *Christus*, felt constrained to write on the manuscript a sentence to the effect that it was his *gift* to her.[12] Liszt also gave other manuscripts to the young woman, including *Am Grabe Richard Wagners* (1883), *Soirées de Vienne*, no. 6 (revised edition, 1882), the *Réminiscences* on Verdi's "Simon Boccanegra" (1882), and the

---

raphy remained for years one of the more authoritative narratives to have been written, and this malicious tale continues to infiltrate itself into the literature. The other side of the story refuting Lina's account lay buried in the Lachmund archives in New York and would not appear until 1995.

11. LL, pp. 319–22.

12. Liszt had given the manuscript to Lina in February 1886, while they were both in Budapest, and she had already assumed the duties of caregiver. The score seems to have been earlier misplaced by Liszt, for the inscription reads: "Aufgefundene Manuscript von Fraülein Schmalhausen, und derselben freundlichst verehrt. F. Liszt, Februar 86, Budapest" (i.e., "The manuscript was located by Fräulein Schmalhausen, and presented most sincerely to the same. F. Liszt").

Mephisto-Polka (1883) which is actually dedicated to her. Once again we observe Liszt's inscription on the manuscript of the *Soirées de Vienne* piece informing us quite plainly that it is "the property of Lina Schmalhausen." Liszt knew full well what he was doing by clearing up the question of proprietary rights in so public a fashion during his lifetime. Lina's ownership of these manuscripts could never be challenged, and she was free to dispose of them as she wished.[13]

III

All this raises a further question: What was the nature of Liszt's relationship with Lina Schmalhausen?

Long before they were reunited in Bayreuth in the summer of 1886, there had been talk of a possible liaison between the pair. In Budapest and Rome, Lina had assumed the duties of virtual housekeeper. This brought her into daily intimate contact with the composer as never before. Liszt's inner circle of friends and pupils could not help but observe that Lina was here, there, and everywhere, tending to "Der Meister's" slightest needs. Moreover, the pair were by now allowing themselves the luxury of such little gestures

13. And dispose of them she did. A few years after Liszt's death and after her return to Berlin, she offered to sell some of these manuscripts to the British Library. After a protracted correspondence, the trustees of the library agreed to buy the manuscript of *Christus* for thirty pounds but declined the others. The unpublished letters between Lina and the British museum trustees are preserved in the British Library under the call number M.S. folio 87.

as embracing and holding hands, and they clearly enjoyed each other's company. Liszt was now in his seventy-fifth year; Lina was twenty-two. She had been his pupil for nearly seven years. For Liszt, we may conjecture that his warm feelings toward Lina were akin to those of an indulgent father toward a favorite daughter—toward one who was now serving him with devotion in his twilight years, subordinating her life to his, and holding his best and highest interests at heart. From Lina's perspective, however, matters looked somewhat different. We have no doubt that she was deeply in love with Liszt—her diary provides abundant evidence of that. But that alone would hardly make her unique: many a female pupil had been in love with Liszt long before Lina came on the scene, and she was intelligent enough to know it. Lina, however, had good reason to suppose that her own situation could not be compared with theirs. Liszt was now ailing. His eyesight was failing rapidly, he could neither read nor write without difficulty; and since he now moved about much more slowly, he needed constant help to put on his clothes and a friendly arm to cross the street. His pupils Arthur Friedheim, August Göllerich, Bernhard Stavenhagen, and others in his entourage during this final year were quick to help, of course, and they often took turns to assist him with correspondence or read aloud to him from the newspapers or from a favorite book. But Lina's contributions were of a different order. She tidied Liszt's apartment, bought and prepared his food, looked after his laundry, and generally made life softer for him. In brief, she provided a woman's touch, and for Liszt that was decisive. Liszt needed

Lina whenever he was away from Weimar; she knew it, and drew solace from it.

In Weimar itself the situation was radically different. For many years the smooth running of Liszt's social life there had been the concern of Baroness Olga von Meyendorff. She was the widow of Baron Felix von Meyendorff, who had been appointed Russian ambassador to the court of Weimar in 1867. Not long after receiving a diplomatic transfer to Karlsruhe, the Baron had died, leaving his thirty-two-year-old widow to look after their four small sons in a strange city. Unable to bear the loneliness of her new life, Olga returned to Weimar, primarily to be near Liszt with whom she had meanwhile struck up a correspondence.[14] Olga and Liszt remained intimate friends for the rest of his life. She often accompanied him on his travels in order to provide a gentler environment for him. And in Weimar it was Olga to whom

---

14. Olga von Meyendorff (née Princess Gortchakova) (1838–1926) always occupied an important place in the Liszt narrative. But it was not until modern times, with the first publication of her large collection of Liszt letters, that the central role she played during his twilight years was revealed—a role she acquired by default, so to speak, once Liszt's former companion, Princess Carolyne von Sayn-Wittgenstein had left Weimar and had moved permanently to Rome. (See Edward Waters, ed., *The Letters of Franz Liszt to Olga von Meyendorff, 1871–1886,* trans. William Tyler [Dumbarton Oaks, 1979].) Liszt had renewed his acquaintance with the Meyendorffs in 1867, the year that Felix had been appointed Russian ambassador to the court of Weimar. The young couple had turned up at a performance of his oratorio *Saint Elisabeth,* in the Wartburg Castle, having first encountered Liszt in Rome a few years earlier. After the early death of Olga's husband, Franz Liszt seems to have been the only man with whom she desired to share any domestic intimacy. In consequence, she aroused the jealousy of many women, including Lina Schmalhausen.

Liszt turned whenever he entertained special guests or put on large dinner parties. She rented a house on Belvedere Allee, almost opposite the Hofgärtnerei, so she could walk across the road and be with Liszt whenever he wished it. Olga was an outstanding hostess, her social skills having been honed through years of experience as the wife of a diplomat. Although the tongues wagged in Weimar, the relationship between Liszt and Baroness von Meyendorff remained platonic.

The Baroness despised Lina Schmalhausen and the feeling was reciprocated. Liszt himself was so worried about their mutual hostility that he tried to make sure that the two women never met in his presence. Lina's diary entry for Tuesday, August 3, the day of his funeral, actually contains the sentence: "During his lifetime the Master never wanted to see us together with him. I did not want it to happen at his coffin either. No sooner had I left than the Baroness arrived."

IV

The sharp decline in Liszt's health during the last three or four years of his life calls for comment because it colors so much of the Schmalhausen narrative. In July 1881, Liszt had fallen down the stairs of the Hofgärtnerei and had injured himself so badly that he was bedridden for several weeks. A local Weimar physician, Dr. Richard Brehme, was consulted, and according to his medical report Liszt suffered from a crushed toe, two fractured ribs, an open wound on his right thigh, the possibility of bruising of the lungs, and pleurisy.[15] Glossed over by Liszt's earlier biographers, this accident, we now realize, was Liszt's traumatic entry into old age. The first ominous signs of dropsy had also appeared, and Liszt's legs had became so bloated that he had taken to wearing a pair of comfortable old slippers in preference to normal dress shoes, which he found constricting. (In a rare outbreak of humour, Princess Carolyne described Liszt's slippers as being so large that you could float from Civitavecchia to Naples in them. And she observed that they made Liszt look like "an old organist.")[16] It was after Liszt's grueling trips to Paris and London in the spring of 1886 that a group of his students who met him at the Weimar railway station in June of that year were shocked to see Miska the manservant emerge from the coach indicating that Liszt's legs were swollen to the point that he would have to be carried from the train. Friedheim, Göllerich, and Alexander Siloti were among those who helped to lift Liszt onto the platform and transport him to a waiting carriage. For much of his adult life Liszt also had to contend with chronic dental problems. For years he had suffered from a chronic gum disease, probably pyorrhea, and many of his teeth had either fallen out or had been extracted. His Budapest dentist, József Árkővy, had made no fewer than three upper dental plates for him, but Liszt found them uncomfortable to wear, with the result that he could hardly chew meat and toward the end was confined to a diet of soft

foods. If we add to these indignities the fact of his near blindness in one eye, the result of a cataract, which constrained his
composing and forced him to dictate much of his correspondence, we begin to understand how vulnerable he was
during the last few months of his life. The cold that he had
taken with him to his drafty rooms in Colpach Castle in Luxembourg, where he stayed as a guest of the Hungarian
painter Mihály Munkácsy in the early part of July 1886, had
developed rapidly, and by the time he reached Bayreuth in
the early hours of July 20, after an all-night journey on the
train sitting next to an open window, he was already suffering from pneumonia, a fact that he himself understood
perfectly well, even though it was slow to dawn on his incompetent Bayreuth doctors.

But there were yet more reasons to arouse Lina's anxiety
for Liszt's welfare. Throughout his life, he had always been
a heavy drinker, but his consumption of alcohol increased
with age. This was doubtless in part a response to the various
aches and pains associated with his symptoms, some of which
were unpleasant. After his accident, he took to drinking ab-
sinthe, a toxic combination of wormwood and alcohol,
whose potentially lethal effects were well known, especially
to the French who had created this exotic libation a generation earlier. During the last few days of his life, Liszt's doctors forbade all alcohol, an obvious enough injunction
under normal circumstances but one that in Liszt's case may
have been a mistake because it was one of his few remaining
pleasures, and he now had to battle with the pangs of with-
drawal along with everything else. Until the last day or two

of his life, Liszt compromised on this advice, mixing water with his wine. Smoking his beloved cigars had long since been abandoned because they brought on bouts of violent coughing that were so debilitating to him.

Hovering over everything else was the unpleasant prospect of an operation for the removal of a cataract on the left eye. The condition had been diagnosed as early as February 1884, and it was confirmed in June 1886 by the celebrated ophthalmologist Alfred Graefe, whom Liszt had visited at his clinic in Halle. Liszt evidently suffered from a "grey cataract," probably of the dense nuclear senile variety, which filters out the color blue while admitting the color red. When, a few weeks earlier, he had written to Lina Schmalhausen instructing her to write to him in large letters and in red ink, he was providing unwitting proof of Graefe's diagnosis.

It was the prospect of blindness that Liszt feared most because it would have brought his work as a composer to an abrupt halt. Alfred Graefe was the obvious choice for the removal of his cataract. Graefe's private clinic in Halle, not far from Weimar, was on the point of becoming world famous. At the time Liszt consulted him, Graefe was beginning to claim an unprecedented success rate. Hitherto, the chief risk for any patient undergoing this kind of surgery was the loss of the eye through postoperative infections. Graefe had pioneered the use of antiseptic techniques at his clinic with staggering results. During the five-year period from 1884 to 1889, the medical record shows that he performed 1,074 cataract operations and lost fewer than ten cases to infection.[17] Alfred Graefe should not be confused with his equally illustrious cousin, Albrecht von Graefe, whose own place in the history of ophthalmology was assured when, a few years earlier, he had designed the so-called Graefe knife, a custom-built scalpel for the swift removal of cataracts. Alfred would have been skilled in the use of his cousin's knife, which required deftness and speed on the part of the surgeon. Most important of all, Alfred was generally acclaimed for his exploratory use of cocaine as a local anesthetic, which removed much of the pain and discomfort until then associated with such operations. This explains Liszt's reassuring remark to Princess Carolyne that the operation would be "quite anodyne."[18]

The telegram that Liszt sent to Lina Schmalhausen once he got to Bayreuth in July 1886, instructing her to leave Carlsbad and join him there, must have brought her both relief and joy. Her precarious situation within the Liszt circle actually prevented her from journeying to Bayreuth without a specific invitation from Liszt. She already knew in advance the date of his arrival, of course, because he had written her a letter from Luxembourg (July 6) giving her a rough outline of his itinerary, and she would have readied herself for a definite summons. But it is clear that Liszt himself wanted to assess the situation in Bayreuth before persuading Lina to make the journey, reserve her accommodations, and brace herself for possible confrontations with those people whom both she and Liszt knew to be unfriendly toward her. Hence

17. These figures may be found in WZ, pp. 398–99.
18. LLB, vol. 7, p. 442.

the last-minute telegram following the earlier letter.[19] Bayreuth was flooded with visitors, and even though Liszt was ill
and needed Lina's attentions, he was also aware that this
young woman had to be protected against gossip and that discretion was a necessary component of the relationship. He
arrived in Bayreuth early on Wednesday morning, July 21;
she arrived late that same evening. Once she had reached
Bayreuth, Liszt also made it his business to compensate her
with some "travel money," which he placed in an anonymous
envelope so that the other students would not observe him.
But observe him they did, and Lina was subsequently regarded by some of them as little better than a kept woman.

V

The dark threads of moral disapproval which are woven
into the texture of Lina's narrative are easy to understand
once we set them within the wider context of Liszt's circle of
students and disciples. Liszt's masterclasses were the focal
point of much more than piano playing. They had never lost
their social origins and were besides a meeting point where
friends, rivals, and even archenemies rubbed shoulders on a
regular basis. These classes, which were by now world famous,

19. It was sent on July 20 (probably from Frankfurt, where Liszt spent the
night before proceeding to Bayreuth), and its terse message ran: "Tomorrow, Wednesday afternoon, arrives and awaits you in Bayreuth—Liszt"
(KFL, p. 542). Lina was expecting the message, and it took her a mere three
hours to travel from Carlsbad to Bayreuth for her reunion with Liszt.

had begun in a modest way in the early 1850s as Sunday afternoon "at homes" where Liszt and his colleagues would get together in Weimar to play chamber music and socialize; Liszt's students of that earlier period—Hans von Bülow, Carl Tausig, Karl Klindworth—would also be encouraged to exhibit their talents, with Liszt making the occasional comment on the performance. From there the classes developed into something more strictly pedagogical, but there was always the sense that Liszt was presiding over a wonderful party for his guests. After Liszt's return from his Roman sojourn, in 1869, the first thing he did was to re-establish his Weimar masterclasses, which were now held three afternoons a week and attracted gifted young men and women from the four quarters. The circle of pupils was often joined by special visitors from out of town—his biographer Lina Ramann, the editor Otto Lessmann, the scholar Marie Lipsius ("La Mara"), the conductor Felix Mottl, the harpist Wilhelm Posse, Liszt's old friend the jurist Dr. Carl Gille; and sometimes even the grand duke and duchess of Weimar themselves would appear. Pauline Apel, Liszt's longtime housekeeper, continued to distribute her home-baked cakes and serve drinks. After the class Liszt would frequently express an interest in playing a game of whist, and more drinks would lubricate the conversation. Quite often, too, Liszt would then proceed to entertain his young charges at one or another of the local Weimar hotels where alcohol would continue to be served. It was not unusual for these parties to break up at one or two o'clock in the morning, the survivors zig-zagging their way along the darkened streets of Weimar, finding their lodgings with difficulty. Then there were the famous summer outings to such places as Jena, Eisenach, Tiefurt, and Leipzig in which Liszt would be accompanied by upward of a dozen of his pupils to attend special concerts. The Jena "sausage parties," put on by Carl Gille in Liszt's honor, were an annual event not to be missed. That there was heavy drinking among some of the young men is beyond dispute. Both Alfred Reisenauer and Arthur Friedheim were rapidly building up a reputation for drinking that was to pursue them throughout their careers. Carl Lachmund once observed Reisenauer down thirteen *Seidl* of heavy Bavarian beers within three hours at the Zum Elephanten hotel in Weimar, a regular meeting place for the group.[20] That was in July 1883 when Reisenauer was nineteen years old. When, a few years later, he embarked on his major concert tours (he is said to have given more than two thousand recitals in his all-too-brief career) he regularly sought consolation in the arms of Bacchus by consuming vast quantities of champagne. In 1907 he died in his hotel room at Libau, in Latvia, in the middle of a concert tour, after a bout of drinking, aged forty-four.

Friedheim's case was more serious still. He was arrested during his first visit to New York, in 1892, and charged with creating an affray in the lobby of the Amberg Theater while inebriated. He spent the night under detention at the East Twenty-second Street Precinct. Before the arrival of the police, he had struck the doorkeeper of the theater on the chest, who later died. Friedheim was then charged with the

20. LL, p. 240.

man's murder. When it was revealed in court that the victim had a history of chronic heart disease, the presiding judge dismissed the charges.[21] Although there is no mention of this tragedy in Friedheim's memoir *Life and Liszt,* the case must have had serious consequences for his career. He was unable to make headway as a performer in New York and left for Chicago where he taught for a while; then he settled in England and held positions at the Guildhall School of Music and the Manchester College of Music. After several unsettled years in Germany he finally returned to America at the outbreak of war, in 1914. All this lay in the future, of course, but there were many who thought that the seeds of such behavior had already been sown in Weimar.

Of all the people who later came forward with critical remarks about Liszt's classes—Walter Damrosch[22] and Clara Schumann[23] especially—it was Emil von Sauer who provided the most poignant comments. Sauer studied with Liszt in 1885 and was disillusioned with some of the people surrounding the master. He later made some intriguing remarks in favor of a life of sobriety. "The habit of taking alcoholic drinks with the idea that they lead to a more fiery performance is a dangerous custom that has been the ruin of more than one pianist. The performer who would be at

21. The case was reported in three separate editions of New York's *Evening World* on April 21, 1892.

22. Damrosch described the class of 1882 as "a pitiful crowd of sycophants and incompetents" (DMML, p. 40).

23. The day after Liszt's death, Clara Schumann wrote in her diary: "He was eminent as a keyboard virtuoso but a dangerous example for the young" (LCS, vol. 3, p. 479).

his best must live a very careful, almost abstemious life. . . . I have watched alcohol tear down in a few years what had taken decades of hard practice and earnest study to build up."[24] Was Sauer thinking of his time at Weimar when he penned these lines? They appeared just a few months after Reisenauer had died. One wonders what Liszt would have made of them. For the rest, Liszt's oft-quoted remark directed against those students who gave straight, well-behaved performances, filled with self-denial, and whose only commitment was to the printed page, takes on a certain piquancy: "You should join a temperance society," he would exclaim. And then, when the awful prospect of such a situation had sunk in, he would add: "but only temporarily."

Lina watched and waited. She was clearly offended by the behavior of some of these young men, whom she perceived to be boisterous, obnoxious, uncaring, and unappreciative of what Liszt was doing to help them. And when Ramann finally asked her to provide an account of Liszt's last ten days, she exploded with venom. The violence of some of her observations will take the Liszt aficionado by surprise. But her side of the story is long overdue, and it deserves to be told.

VI

Given the many complexities of Lina's place within Liszt's inner circle, we come to the most difficult question of all:

24. STCP, p. 763.

How truthful is her account of Liszt's illness and death in Bayreuth?

We believe her to be absolutely reliable in the presentation of the facts, which can be corroborated from other sources—the names of pupils and colleagues who visited the dying composer on particular days, an outline of the conversations they had, the comings and goings at Wahnfried and the Bayreuth Festival Theatre, and even the symptomology of Liszt's terminal illness. Where we must exercise caution is with Lina's interpretation of those facts. Her narrative is sometimes colored by the dark motives and intentions she attributes to those individuals who openly disliked her and were disliked by her in turn. She was highly protective of Liszt's interests; and whenever she felt that those interests were being threatened, either through carelessness or selfishness even within Liszt's family circle, she did not hesitate to express herself in the strongest language. Wagner's prose works, which were inflicted on the dying Liszt in a series of forced readings at his bedside, are described as "rubbish"; Eva Wagner, Liszt's granddaughter, is depicted as "this monster of a grandchild"; Cosima's last-minute concern for her father's illness is characterized as "an act"; while Dr. Karl Landgraf, the Wagner family physician who treated Liszt during his final hours and may have hastened his death, is memorably called "the bungler of Bayreuth." The Wagners would have been aghast to read such language. No wonder that the diary was suppressed.

Lina's account of Liszt's death is so graphic, and filled with details so wrenching, that no modern chronicler could enhance the drama. She is our only source for the wretched business of the botched attempt to embalm the body—an episode that was carefully concealed from posterity and remained largely unknown to generations of biographers. And it is from Lina, too, that we learn that the transfer of Liszt's body to Wahnfried was made by Cosima and Wagner's old factotum Bernhard Schnappauf, who had to lift the bloated remains and place them in a metal coffin, which they then pushed across the road from Siegfriedstrasse on a handcart. And all this on a busy Monday morning (August 2, 1886) in Bayreuth, and in full view of the usual curiosity seekers, an omnipresent aspect of any Wagner festival. We will leave to Schmalhausen the task of telling, in her own way, the rest of this part of her gripping story. Above all, it is thanks to Schmalhausen that we know of Liszt's desperation at being taken ill in Bayreuth and of his growing knowledge that he was to meet his maker there. "If only I do not die here," was his constant refrain. Neglected by his daughter, his illness trivialized by his grandchildren, Liszt was likened during his final hours to King Lear by Schmalhausen, an image that has come to haunt the literature. That Liszt's death was a bitter personal blow for her goes without saying. And that she blamed Cosima and the Wagners for neglecting Liszt is writ large on every page. She later memorialized Liszt in the following words: "He was the light of my existence, he lifted and ennobled my thoughts, he was my creator, yes, my whole world."[25]

25. MSD, p. 175.

Six weeks after Liszt's funeral, Lina came back to Bayreuth. The Wagner festival had ended, the crowds had dispersed, and the town had lapsed once more into sleepy inactivity. She entered the room in which he had died and noted that everything had been changed. The floors had been washed and waxed, new furniture had been installed, and even the old wallpaper had been torn down. Everything possible had been done to remove the stench of death. Both Cosima and Princess Carolyne, Liszt's old companion, had sent Frau Fröhlich one hundred marks to compensate her for the "inconvenience" of having Liszt die on her premises. Lina then visited Liszt's grave. It still lacked a headstone. There was only a simple cross of ivy and some flowers decorating the newly turned earth. Everything looked makeshift. In fact, nobody yet knew where the body would finally rest. Even before it had been lowered into the ground, requests had reached Bayreuth to have the body moved to Budapest or to Weimar, both of which cities had a powerful claim on Liszt. But Cosima harbored a secret desire: to have her father remain in Bayreuth under Wagner's shadow. And as his closest living relative, it was Cosima's will that prevailed.

VII

Schmalhausen, like everybody else, was doubtless appalled at the monumental quarrel that broke out over the "ownership" of the body. The competing claims for the corpse were symptomatic of darker motives, however, not immediately obvious. They had to do with the "ownership" of the life, and the extent to which that life would be bound to Bayreuth. The drama that unfolded during the months following Liszt's death equaled any that he had experienced during his lifetime. Among the chief players were the Grand Duke of Weimar, the Hungarian government, and Bayreuth itself. We have reserved for the epilogue the telling of this story.

After Liszt's death Lina Schmalhausen held a brief professorship in music education at the Budapest National Conservatory of Music. In 1891 she received an invitation to return to the Berlin Royal Court, in order to supervise the instruction of the younger members of the royal family and was given the title of "Royal Prussian Court Pianist." To some extent, then, her life had come full circle. Her later years were marked by illness and privation. In 1889, and again in 1892, she offered some of her precious Liszt manuscripts for sale to the British Library, explaining that she had got herself into "a little money difficulty."[26] The Library gave her the paltry sum of thirty pounds for the oratorio *Christus*, rejecting her offer to sell them the "Gondola" piano pieces and *Am Grabe Richard Wagners* which eventually went to other buyers.

In the summer of 1927 Lina entered a Berlin hospital and had her right leg amputated. She was treated as a "third class" patient and placed in a ward with thirty other patients. Such was her poverty that she was unable to pay for an arti-

26. British Library, M.S. folio 87. The letter from Schmalhausen to the Trustees of the British Library, concerning the sale of the manuscript of *Christus* was published in WFL, vol. 3, p. 433.

ficial limb, which cost between 300 and 400 marks. Word of her plight was received by Emma Grosskurth, one of Liszt's students who had known Lina well in the old days. Emma contacted a number of Liszt's former students with a request to send donations to the hospital to pay for Lina's treatment.[27] She died the following year, supported in death by some of the very people by whom she had felt rejected in life. To be a pupil of Liszt was to belong to a charmed circle of musicians who revered the memory of his magical presence long after he had gone to the grave. They helped Lina because Liszt would have helped her, as he had helped them all.

27. CLC, series 1, folder 49.

Liszt's Last Days

The Diary of Lina Schmalhausen

Thursday, July 22

I was awakened early by the chambermaid, dressed myself neatly, and with little Belli[1] went to the beloved Master at no. 1, Siegfriedstrasse. When I rang the outer door, a maid opened it and said that Herr Dr. was probably not yet ready to receive visitors. I did not even let her finish: at 7:30 A.M. the Master was always up. I went first into the salon and because no one was there, and I heard voices coming from the next room, I opened the door to the bedchamber where I saw the beloved Master talking with Göllerich[2] and Miska,[3]

1. The name of Lina Schmalhausen's lapdog.

2. August Göllerich (1859–1923) had joined Liszt's circle as a piano student in 1884. A devoted teacher and pedagogue, he wrote an influential book on Liszt (Berlin, 1908) which contains one of the better catalogs of the composer's music. He also compiled a detailed account of Liszt's masterclasses for the years 1884–86, which was published posthumously as *Franz Liszts Klavierunterricht von 1884–86,* ed. Wilhelm Jerger (Regensburg, 1975). See GLK.

3. Mihály ("Miska") Kreiner was a Hungarian who had entered Liszt's service in 1884. He was the last of a series of trusted manservants and valets who had looked after Liszt for the last seventeen years of his life. The duties of these worthies included setting out Liszt's clothes, shaving him, announcing visitors, running various errands, and accompanying him on foreign travel. Miska Kreiner should not be confused with Miska Sipka, an earlier manservant, who had died in 1875.

who was combing his hair at the washstand; I literally threw myself into his arms; he did not immediately recognize me under my hat and veil and was embarrassed for a moment. Then he called out, "Ah, Lina!" He kept drawing me to him delightedly; then he allowed himself to be dressed in his velvet coat because he was still standing there in his shirtsleeves. In the meantime I greeted Göllerich. The Master said, "Now Lina, you still have much to tell me." He took my arm and led me down a few steps into the garden. Göllerich followed, the Master walking up and down the small garden with me. Belli attracted attention, for the Master was surprised to see a dog in my company. He inquired after its name ("So, Belli," he remarked), asked how I had acquired it and for how much, and thought that twenty guilders was quite inexpensive because in Paris these little dogs cost much more, and that he knew because Mme [Cécile] Munkácsy[4] owned several of them. The Master inquired where I had alighted, how long it had taken to travel from Carlsbad to Bayreuth, and would not believe that the distance could be covered in only three hours. The Master looked as if he were suffering a great deal and coughed terribly. We stood with Göllerich in

4. Cécile Munkácsy (1845–1915) was the wealthy wife of the Hungarian painter Mihály von Munkácsy (1844–1900), whose oil painting of Liszt in old age is one of the finest ever executed. Lina Schmalhausen harbored a great dislike of this portrait (see p. ii). Earlier in the year, in April, Liszt had been a guest of the Munkácsys at their sumptuous home in Paris. Later he had visited them at Colpach Castle, their residence in Luxembourg. The last photograph ever taken of Liszt (c. July 19) shows him on the arm of Mme Munkácsy. The alert observer will not fail to notice in the background one of her small dogs mentioned by Liszt—a Brussels Griffon. From Colpach, Liszt had journeyed straight to Bayreuth.

the bedroom, who did not even have the courtesy to leave me alone to speak with the Master for a few moments. Therefore, the Master said, "Lina, one moment please," and went with me into the salon. He closed the door behind him, and we stood at the end of the room, by the entrance; there he embraced me warmly and said, "How happy I am to see you again; it refreshes me to know that you are here. Everything is healthy and well here" (he now pulled a face as if he felt repulsed by something) and added, "It is nothing debilitating [*ausgemergeltes*]."

"I wanted to tell you that we can see each other for only a week. Tomorrow one of your sponsors, [Adelheid von] Schorn,[5] is arriving; this does not matter, but after that it is impossible. I am only telling you this because of the arrangements when you are renting the apartment. I had considered—first this, then that—where we could meet, but I always came back to Bayreuth; this was the only way out. One week will at least give us the chance for a little reunion. I sent you a telegram immediately, so that you would not lose any time. Baroness von Meyendorff will arrive on the 2nd or 3rd of August; and so you'll leave a day earlier."[6]

5. Adelheid von Schorn (1841–1916) was the daughter of the art historian Ludwig von Schorn and Henrietta von Schorn, a lady-in-waiting to the Grand Duchess Maria Pawlowna at the Court of Weimar. She had lived in Weimar all her life, was a frequent visitor to the Hofgärtnerei, and was a confidante of Princess Carolyne von Sayn-Wittgenstein. Her two books *Zwei Menschenalter* (1901) and *Das Nachklassiche Weimar* (1911–12) contain some vivid pen sketches of Liszt. The former book also gives an account of this particular visit to Bayreuth and of Liszt's death there (SZM, pp. 466–67).

6. This was by now a well-rehearsed procedure. Exactly the same choreography had been adopted during the Bayreuth Festival of 1884: Lina had

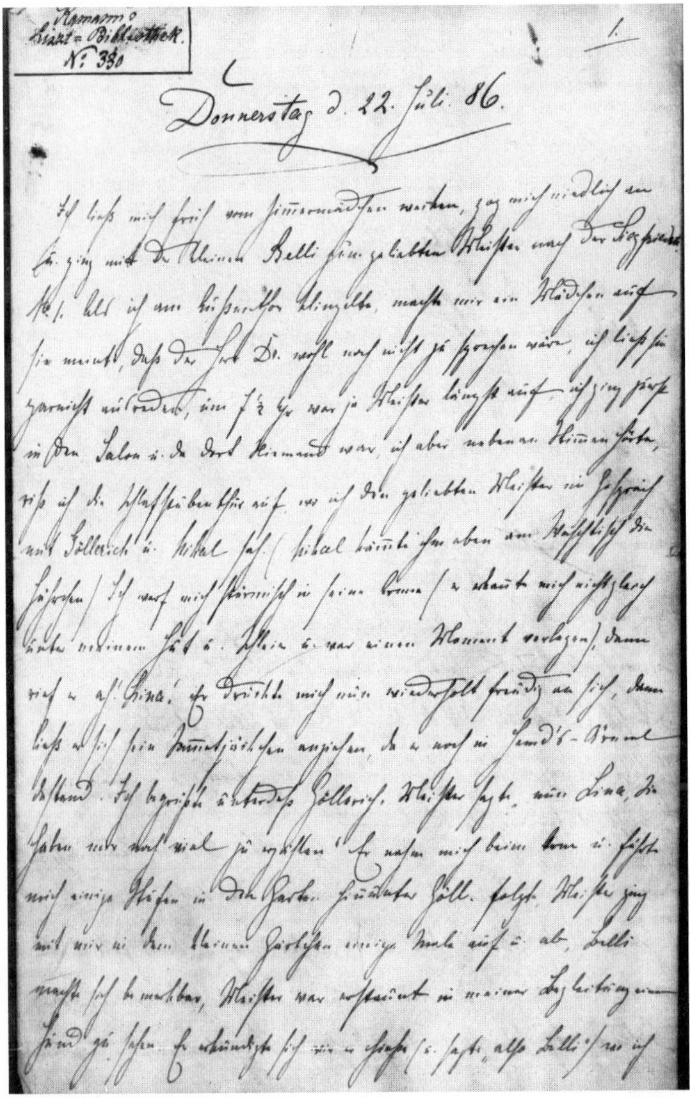
Liszt-Bibliothek.
N: 330
1.
Donnerstag d. 22. Juli 86.

"I was awakened early by the chambermaid." Thursday, July 22, 1886.

I answered that I could leave in a couple of days, that I had only come to Bayreuth to see him again and be allowed to embrace him once more. Liszt said, "No, that would be too short for *me*. I want to have you stay longer." The Master also remarked that I had become a little slimmer and went back with me into the bedroom, where Göllerich stood. The Master inquired whether I had already taken coffee. When I replied yes, he said, "You old eavesdropper, you can't stop snooping.[7] Miska, have some coffee made at once." He then asked me how long I had been in Carlsbad, whether I had also taken the waters, etc. Then he showed me his small gold pencil, his white mother-of-pearl knife, and the little tooth-pick all of which I had given him years ago. He was never without these things; he asked for them every morning. The toothpick and the lead pencil always had to be in his vest pocket, the knife in the pocket of his trousers; when erasing his letters and notes he used only my knife. He dubbed them his "Lina-knife" and "Lina-pencil" [*"Lina-Messer"* and *"Lina-Blei"*], and when one of these objects happened to be mis-placed he became *most* vehement, and the search had to

arrived in Bayreuth in mid-July to be with Liszt and she had left a day or two before Baroness Meyendorff arrived in early August. This ballet had always been danced to perfection, until the music stopped.

7. This reference to Lina as an eavesdropper ("eine Auglauscherin") has already been dealt with on page 6. Liszt well knew that the other students called her "Miss Telltale," and it explains the present conversation. The best way to deflate the gossip ballooning around Lina, he must have thought, was to puncture it with the needle of irony. He is making a pointed joke at Göllerich's expense, articulating the absurd idea that Lina had been secretly sipping her coffee behind the closed door while listening to the harmless conversation he had earlier been having with Göllerich.

continue until the knife and pencil were found. During all these past years he always showed me the pencil and the knife immediately after our first embrace, just as he did now. He looked at me with a searching glance and said, "This is how one honors precious keepsakes." Then he returned with Göllerich and me to the salon.

As we were sitting and chatting, Cosima entered, dressed in deepest mourning, a thick, black veil shrouding her face. She acted as if she had not seen me. The Master said in French, "You see, I have visitors early in the morning, Fräulein Schmalhausen" (pointing in my direction). "I recommended her to you most warmly in Palermo, some time ago.[8] And here is Göllerich. I always refer to him as 'the vegetarian,' and also present him to others by that name." Cosima silently nodded her head and acted as if we were invisible. The situation became awkward, and I told the Master that I wanted to leave. He answered that there was no need to leave, but when he saw that Cosima expressed no words of support he said all right, but please to come back soon. I then patrolled up and down the garden with Göllerich. After an hour, the poor Master was free. He was visibly pleased to find me still there, and I now drank coffee in his salon; he then went with us back into the bedroom and sat down at his worktable. There he wrote a few lines to Mme

8. Cosima and Richard Wagner had sojourned in Palermo in the early part of 1882. Liszt was in Rome for much of January of that same year; but nowhere in the literature is there mention of him crossing the Tyrrhenian Sea to visit the Wagners in the Sicilian capital, much less in Schmalhausen's company. Perhaps the "recommendation" took place by letter.

Munkácsy and enclosed a catalog of the [Bayreuth] per-
formers, also a few lines to Countess Zamoyska[9] with the
comment that he would remain in Bayreuth until the 9th of
next month. (He told me, "I will certainly have left by then,
but that doesn't matter.") Then I had to sit at the desk with
him. Göllerich sat beside me like an adhesive plaster. The
Master had Miska bring the photographs of M. and Mme.
Munkácsy for me to look at. As I regarded her portrait he
said, "This picture was taken by our Koller in Pest.[10] Mme
Munkácsy said that he charged her an awful lot for it; she
looks very theatrical here, incidentally." I had the little dog
on my lap. The Master said, "In Luxembourg there was always this eternal fussing with the dogs. In Paris the smallest
dog of the Munkácsys ran away; she offered a reward of a
hundred francs and got him back. The little thing had
caught an awful cold, however, and was very ill; it was sent to
the hospital for a fortnight where she paid a further 3 francs
a day as well. After a fortnight the fellow dies."

The Master now repeatedly asked Göllerich to attend to
the letters, and whether he did not know of any mailbox in
the area. But Göllerich was hard of hearing; he thought that
Miska could take care of the letters later. The Master asked

9. The Polish Countess Ludmilla Gizycka-Zamoyska was a lady-in-waiting
to Duchess Sophie at the Viennese court. She was an amateur composer of
songs and salon pieces for piano, whose public performances Liszt had
helped to arrange in Vienna, in April 1881. A number of her compositions
are listed in his Budapest music library (see EFLE, vol. 1, pp. 193–94).

10. "Our Koller" refers to Károly Koller (1823?–90), the Hungarian photographer who had taken the well-known photograph of Lina and Liszt together in Budapest the previous year (see page xiv).

him at least to hand the letters to Miska, which he then did. The Master now embraced me and said, "He would do better to leave us alone, but he is a good fellow and I don't want to hurt his feelings today by sending him away." Göllerich returned promptly at 9:00 A.M. Eva[11] entered and said, "Grandpapa, I only came to tell you that I have some errands to run in the town for Mama and can't come to you before 11:00 A.M." When she had gone, the Master said, "She is a lively, determined young thing; she doesn't resemble the others over there[12] at all." He asked me, "Doesn't my daughter seem very changed and thin to you? Yes, over there only sorrow exists!" (pointing with his hand to Wahnfried). "She has astonishing willpower and energy. Just imagine, she has taken up quarters right at the top [of the Bayreuth Theatre] and the children live by themselves at Wahnfried. She arrives early, sometimes already at 6:00 A.M., and takes coffee with me, which she brings over with her; then she spends all day up there.[13] She has fabulous energy."

After writing, the Master was tired. He sat down at his special invalid chair (the feet stretching out on a footstool). Terrible. Four months ago, in Pest, he was still just like a God; now he was completely broken. He wanted to try to sleep a

11. Eva Wagner (1867–1942) was the nineteen-year-old daughter of Richard and Cosima Wagner, and Liszt's granddaughter.

12. "Over there" was Liszt's ironic euphemism for Wahnfried, the home of the Wagner family, which lay on the opposite side of the street, and where he had always been an honored guest in the old days before Wagner's death, three years earlier.

13. "Up there," by contrast, was Liszt's way of referring to the Bayreuth Theatre.

little; Göllerich read something aloud. I sat beside the Master on the green chaise lounge. I covered the Master's feet with his old grey plaid and placed Belli between the Master's feet. Belli made himself comfortable in the plaid and lay between the Master's feet, as if in a cradle. The Master stroked the animal's little tail and said, "At least I still have a small pastime!" (his tone was very sad, his expression gloomy). The Master related, while coughing incessantly, that he had been in Halle, and that Volkmann[14] had told him after an examination that he had a little water in the feet. The Master had replied, "Just come right out with it. I have dropsy!" The Master's magnificent face became ever more gloomy at that, and *infinitely* sad.

Göllerich continued to read but could not continue for any length of time because the Master continually coughed, and his whole body shook violently. His head became blood-red and he probably spat out four handkerchiefs of phlegm during two hours. The Master attempted to sleep, but his cough prevented it. When we thought that he had dozed off, Göllerich stopped reading. Then the Master said, "Well, go on, I'm listening," so Göllerich continued to read. Later, at 10:30 A.M., Stavenhagen[15] arrived with his strange, smug

14. Dr. Richard von Volkmann (1830–89) was the head of surgery at Halle. Liszt had consulted him in June, when Volkmann had prescribed a water cure at Bad Kissingen, to precede the operation for removal of a cataract of the left eye recommended by Dr. Alfred Graefe of the same hospital. This cure had already been scheduled for August, immediately following Liszt's visit to Bayreuth; the operation itself was scheduled to take place at Halle in September, but his death intervened. See pp. 86–87.

15. Bernhard Stavenhagen (1862–1914) had joined Liszt's circle of

smile. The Master said that he had played billiards brilliantly in Luxembourg. Then, "Isn't it true, Stavenhagen, that I've suffered for over a week from this miserable cough? Please give me a spoonful of medicine; it is up on the stove." Stavenhagen lovelessly *thrust* a spoon into his mouth. The divine Master feared that he had spilled everything and looked at his vest sorrowfully with a childlike, fearful glance.

I took the Master's watch from his vest pocket, and because it was 12 o'clock I rose to leave. As I was putting on my gloves the Master said, "Those are Carlsbader, I know; the gloves there are superb." I was surprised and inquired when was he in Carlsbad. He replied, "With the Princess [Wittgenstein]; she needed treatment there."[16]

Liszt said that he would shortly be picked up to have lunch at Princess Hatzfeldt's[17] and would not be back before 4:00

---

pupils the previous year. He had soon become an indispensable member of the retinue, had started to perform a number of personal services for the master, and had accompanied him to Budapest, Rome, London, and Luxembourg. While in London, Stavenhagen had made his British debut in Prince's Hall, on April 16, 1886, in an all-Liszt recital at which Liszt himself was present. In 1898 he became court conductor in Weimar, a position that Liszt himself had held in the 1850s.

16. Liszt's memory was correct. Between 1849 and 1853 the princess had taken a series of water cures at Bad Eilsen and Carlsbad. It had been a stressful period in Liszt's own life, too, and one which he had good cause to remember because the illness of the Princess (a form of blood poisoning) had frequently obliged him to commute between Bad Eilsen and Weimar, where he served as court kapellmeister-in-extraordinary. These episodes are related in WFL, vol. 2, pp. 73, 139, 165, and 231.

17. Princess Marie von Hatzfeld (1820–97) was the widow of Prince Friedrich von Hatzfeldt-Trachenberg (1808–74), her second husband. She was a friend of both Liszt and Wagner and was a loyal supporter of the

P.M., so I should return around 4:30 P.M. He accompanied me to the door and kissed my cheek. I now went to the hotel, packed my things, and moved to my previous apartment (Richard Wagner Strasse).[18] There I ate a little something for lunch and went to sleep. Around 4:00 P.M. I went to Siegfriedstrasse. Miska said that the Master had left a message that I should wait because he had some gentlemen visitors at that moment. After half an hour it became too long for me. I heard that Lessmann[19] was there also, and for him

---

Bayreuth Festivals. Her daughter was the attractive Princess Marie ("Mimi") von Schleinitz (1842–1912), a devoted Liszt admirer who, like her mother, was now widowed and was present in Bayreuth during these difficult days. Liszt makes a glancing reference in Schmalhausen's supplement for July 22 to the possibility of Mimi von Schleinitz contracting a second marriage. Schmalhausen writes, "The Master said of Frau [Marie] von Schleinitz: 'Mimi got married with double assurance because her husband, in the hour of his death, wanted her to marry Wolkenstein. Whether she will now assume the same position in Berlin is questionable.'" Marie's late husband was Baron Alexander von Schleinitz (1807–85), a Prussian minister of state, who was twenty-five years her senior. The baron had died the previous year, leaving her widowed at the age of forty-three. Liszt's prediction of a second marriage for the countess turned out to be absolutely correct. She wed Count Anton Wolkenstein-Trostburg (1832–1918) just a few weeks after Liszt's own death.

18. By her "previous apartment," Lina was referring to the one she had occupied on her last visit to the Bayreuth Festival, in the summer of 1884.

19. Otto Lessmann (1844–1918), the owner and editor of the influential *Allgemeine Musik-Zeitung* (1882–1907), was a staunch supporter of both Liszt and Wagner. He was a regular visitor to the Bayreuth Festivals and gave generous coverage to the annual gatherings of the *Allgemeiner Deutscher Musikverein,* of which Liszt was the lifetime president. Liszt thought well of Lessman as a composer and transcribed his three "Tannhäuser" songs for solo piano (S.498).

When Lina writes that she would not have waited for Lessmann "for even

I would not have waited for even one minute. I entered, and to my surprise found no strangers there at all. Stavenhagen, Göllerich, Lessmann, etc. were inside. The Master approached me, kissed my forehead, and said, "We have been waiting for you for a long time, dear Lina." He showed me to a place beside him on the sofa and wanted me to participate in a game of whist. My mood was already unhappy enough, however, and I replied that I had forgotten how to play whist, that I would rather watch. I remained beside the Master and arranged his cards for him.

A variety of things were discussed. I served the Master's wine, or rather his "water," as he did not want even to see wine anymore. Cigars were not allowed either; he had lost his taste for them. Somebody remarked that [Eugène] d'Albert[20] was in Bayreuth. The Master said, "I don't know why he totally ignores me and does not look me up." I noticed his unfavorable reaction. Already in Sondershausen I had

---

one minute," her brusque dismissal of the distinguished critic can only be understood in the context of her disastrous performance of Liszt's A major Concerto at Karlsruhe a couple of years earlier and Lessmann's round condemnation of it (AMZ, no. 24 [June 1885]: p. 218). See also page 5.

20. Eugène d'Albert (1864–1932) had joined Liszt's Weimar masterclass in May 1882, as a youth of eighteen, and had created a sensation with his mastery of the keyboard and his phenomenal sight-reading. Liszt dubbed him "Albertus Magnus," and followed his career with special interest. D'Albert's private life was a stormy one, best reflected in his seven marriages. He embarked upon matrimony while young and was already a father at the time Lina writes of him. It is said that when d'Albert went to register the birth of his firstborn, in Eisenach, the elderly clerk peered over his spectacles and said to the slight young man standing before him, "The father himself must come to report it" (LL, p. 282).

committed a similar blunder when I asked the Master if he was happy with the performance of his symphony in Leipzig, and he had replied indignantly, "My symphony has been performed 10–12 times in the largest cities such as London, Paris, Berlin, etc." I said, "*Tanto meglio*" ["so much better"].[21]

Now Dingeldey[22] arrived with his director, and the Master gave him short shrift. The Master told me in front of Lessmann, "When we are alone I must tell you something about

21. The blunder to which Schmalhausen refers took place the previous month, during a conversation in Sondershausen, when they were both in attendance for the annual festival of the Tonkünstler Versammlung. She had been brash enough to seek his opinion of a recent performance of his "Faust" Symphony given in Leipzig under the direction of the young Arthur Nikisch, for which Nikisch had actually received a standing ovation (FLL, p. 163). But Liszt did not want to extend any gratitude whatsoever to the Leipzig public, which had been hostile to him and his music for many years. Their appreciation, he considered, he could well live without.

22. Ludwig Dingeldey, an American pupil of Liszt who was also an amateur actor, was known to the Weimar circle as "Mr. Sponger" because he was continually seeking loans from Liszt and others, which he then failed to repay. This explains why Liszt gave him "short shrift," in Schmalhausen's words. Dingeldey's aspirations to pursue a career on the stage had evidently reached a point where he could now boast of having a "director." Carl Lachmund got to know Dingeldey in Weimar and was particularly harsh on his character, writing in his diary, "Many kings had their court fool, and this is what this actor is to the Master" (LL, p. 112, fn. 8). As early as October 1878, Liszt had told Olga von Meyendorff dryly, "Dingeldey is not one of *my* first-class pianists; but he has a good presence, maintains good relations with the press, and thus does not have to bother about a recommendation from me. *Pontius* Lassen can send him back to *Pilate* Loën" (WLLM, p. 319). This was a witty reference to the uncertainty hovering over Dingeldey's talents: Eduard Lassen was the music director at Weimar, while Baron August Loën was the intendant of the Weimar Court Theatre—a tug-of-war between music and drama.

the good Madame Jaëll:[23] she is angry with me." We played whist in this fashion until 7:30 P.M., then the Master bade all the gentlemen goodbye and asked me to stay. "I have a few things to tell you that are better not recorded." After everybody had left the Master said, "I just wanted to give you the money for the tickets. Ask Göllerich to get them for you." We remained seated on the green sofa, and the Master said, "Stavenhagen had no reason to regret that he accompanied me along the way; he made many lucrative contacts, and he was well received in London and also played well."[24]

The Master then told me the following: "Imagine, a few days prior to my departure from Weimar, Frau Friedheim[25] comes to me, requesting a confidential conversation, saying that my life depended on her message. I requested that she tell me the news immediately, time was short, and I did not feel like taking an hour for her idle chatter. She asserted very

23. The French pianist Marie Jaëll (née Trautmann) (1846–1925), who had joined Liszt's circle two or three years earlier, was the widow of pianist Alfred Jaëll (1832–82). She was also well known as a composer, having written a large quantity of piano music and a symphonic poem *Ossiane* which had been given its first performance in Paris, in 1879. In later years she became a respected teacher, her best-known pupil being Albert Schweitzer.

24. Stavenhagen had accompanied Liszt on his long trip to Paris and London earlier in the year. See n. 15.

25. Annette Friedheim (d. 1892) was the mother of Arthur Friedheim (1859–1932) who had accompanied her son from St. Petersburg to Weimar when he had joined Liszt's class in 1878 as a youth of nineteen. She had been widowed after only a year of marriage, when her husband, an officer in the Russian Imperial Army, had been killed in Asia. She now devoted all her energy to the upbringing of her only son, was his constant companion and a regular member of Liszt's circle.

decisively that she had to speak with me in private, however, and even behind locked doors. She said that she went bathing with her son and Dayas[26] every morning at 5 o'clock; therefore, she wanted to come to me at 6 o'clock. No sooner said than done.[27] She arrived punctually, locked the door of the Hofgärtnerei behind her, and warned me about seeing a young girl again in Bayreuth who is very dear to my heart, whom I usually invited, and who would come and demand that I marry her. And if I were to refuse, the girl would murder me right here in Bayreuth. I pleaded with her to tell me

---

Arthur Friedheim was extremely close to Liszt, serving as his secretary and general factotum in Weimar, Rome, and Budapest. He took over much of Liszt's letter writing when Liszt's eyesight began to fail. After Liszt's death, he moved to Leipzig where he married. In 1891 the Friedheims moved to New York but his career foundered there, and in 1897 he moved to London where he became a professor of piano at the Guildhall School of Music. After some years in Germany, Friedheim moved back to New York where he became widely known as a champion of Liszt and his music. See the photograph on p. 63.

26. William Humphrys Dayas was an American pupil of Liszt, born in New York City. He had been a member of Liszt's circle since 1883. Friedheim and Dayas were close companions, and Friedheim actually succeeded Dayas as head of the piano department at the Manchester College of Music when Dayas died prematurely, aged forty.

27. Frau Friedheim seems to be making reference to her dawn visits to the Weimar public swimming baths, which used to be situated not far from the present-day ones on Schwanseestrasse. In 1884 they had been improved and opened to bathers of both sexes. They lay within comfortable walking distance of the Hofgärtnerei. Refreshed from her cold plunge, Frau Friedheim doubtless thought she was better able to brace herself for what she knew would be a difficult confrontation with Liszt, who was always up and about at that hour.

the name of the lady, and she said that I must know exactly for whom I felt some interest. I asked, do you perhaps mean Fraülein Schmalhausen? She said yes, you will die because of her in Bayreuth." Thereupon I asked her to leave me in peace, for I saw that the good person was having another one of her foolish ideas.

Turning toward me the Master said, "Well, well, Lina, so I am to die because of you, but I did not try to avoid you, and I invited you to Bayreuth."

I was completely amazed by this news, which affected me more than unpleasantly. The Master looked deathly ill. Suddenly the uncanny idea occurred to me that if he were actually to die here, and I were coincidentally to be alone with him, and he fell asleep while in my care, would not everyone suspect me of being his murderer and believe [Mme] Friedheim? The Master probably noticed how embarrassed I was by his news, for he said that had he known that the idiocy of this fool would annoy me in any way he would not have told me at all. "By the way, tell *no one* what I have just told you." He said this very decisively.

Siegfried[28] now came to fetch his grandfather for dinner.

28. Liszt's grandson Siegfried Wagner (1869–1930) was now seventeen years old. He had spent a lot of time in Liszt's company in Venice, in the winter of 1882–83, not long before Wagner's death. Liszt dubbed the young man "Sigius," a fact we glean from the affectionate portrait of his grandfather that Siegfried left to posterity in his "Erinnerungen" (1923). At first he was attracted to the study of architecture, but after travels to India and China he decided to devote himself to music and studied with Hans Richter and Julius Kniese. After Cosima withdrew from the duties of running the Bayreuth Festival in 1906, it was Siegfried on whom his father's mantle was to fall, and he directed every Bayreuth Festival until his death, almost a quar-

I remained with Siegfried while he played with Belli. The Master got dressed to go over there, then he called me into his bedroom, gave me an envelope, and said that it was for the tickets, plus a little extra to put aside for a rainy day, which I have still left over. He pressed my hand and went into the salon to Siegfried who took his arm and led him to Wahnfried.

Since my living arrangements were temporarily disorganized, I wanted to give Belli to Miska to look after during the night. The Master said, "No, put him into the bed with me." This I did; I placed my little dog into the Master's bed and went home. I felt infinitely sad, could not eat anything for dinner, and went to bed straight away. During the night there was a terrible storm, and I could not sleep.

---

ter of a century later. A gifted conductor and composer, Siegfried always labored under the shadow of his father, although today he has a number of posthumous admirers who are pressing the case to see him recognized in his own right. His list of works is substantial and includes seventeen operas and a number of symphonic works.

Friday, July 23

I got to Siegfriedstrasse early, at 7:00 A.M., and went first to Miska, as Cosima was still with the Master; she left around 8:00 A.M. Miska told me that the Master had not slept all night because of Belli, that the naughty animal had barked constantly. Miska was especially angry at Stavenhagen and thought that he had little love for the Master. At the Munkác-sys in Luxembourg he had regularly slept in until 10:00 A.M. Stavenhagen's room had been across from the Master's. The Master as usual had been up since 5:00 A.M., but because of his bad eyes it had been impossible for him to write or read, so he probably went to Stavenhagen's bedroom at least five times to ask him to get up; but then Stavenhagen would make a special point of continuing his sleep. In short, Miska would not calm down about the ungratefulness of Staven-hagen. Now, after Cosima left, the Master came into Miska's room to see whether I was there. Miska brought coffee for me and Göllerich into the salon. I asked Göllerich to leave me alone with Liszt, at least for five minutes, since I had something to tell him.

I went to the Master in the salon and told him that I wanted to leave [Bayreuth], that I had been thinking about

Freitag den 23 Juli.

"I got to Siegfriedstrasse early." Friday, July 23, 1886.

his comments yesterday regarding Frau Friedheim, that an accident could befall him here, and that in the end I would be branded as his murderess. The Master answered, "Remain calm, the woman is known to be crazy. Had I realized that you would take it at all seriously, I would never have told you. I thought that you would laugh about it."

Now Göllerich entered, and the Master instructed him to procure for me two tickets to *Parsifal* and *Tristan*. "Settle that with Göllerich, dear Lina," he said. "I could request [complimentary] tickets from over there, but with such a sacrificial enterprise, I would get a bad conscience."[29]

The Master always drank water with just a little wine. He was very weak and coughed continually. The Master said to Göllerich: "Have Miska give you 60 marks for the tickets and charge it to my account." I now wanted to hand Göllerich the money which the Master had already given me yesterday for the tickets. Göllerich did not take it, however, and left. The Master then went back to his bedroom and sat down in the middle of the room in his convalescent chair. I wanted to return the envelope to him, and I said, "Dear Master, yesterday you gave me money for the tickets, and when I wanted to give it to Göllerich just now, he did not want to take it." The Master opened the envelope, looked to see if the 100 marks were still inside, and said, "Keep it, you know that I

29. The performance of *Parsifal* took place that same evening, Friday, July 23; the performance of *Tristan* followed on Sunday, July 25. Liszt's comments make it clear that although he was a guest of honor at Bayreuth, he neither asked for nor received complimentary tickets. The festival had always lost money and was now in debt. See p. 189.

don't like any kind of confusion. Before you leave you will receive some travel money as well." I did not want to accept the money at all, but he became angry and searched my dress until he had found my pocket and let the money slip inside.

He then told me the following story about Gille. "Imagine, about three weeks ago I had to go to a church concert in Jena with the Baroness [Meyendorff]. I went to see Gille, and who should open the door for me? Fräulein Spierling.[30] At first I thought that she was visiting him, but far from it. She lives there with him. You can imagine the surprise of the Baroness, the old reprobate succumbing to such foolishness at his age. I had no idea about this improvement; Gille had told me nothing. She is quite a designing person." In my stupidity I asked without thinking what Spierling was actually doing there. The Master echoed slyly, "Yes, what is she doing there? Gille accompanied me with her by train for a part of the way back to Weimar, and then the two of them walked cozily arm in arm back to Jena. I don't mind if he amuses

30. The Jena concert took place on June 25 and consisted of a performance of Mendelssohn's oratorio *St. Paul*.

Anna Spierling was a local student who had attended Liszt's Weimar masterclasses during 1882–83 and was now evidently living with Liszt's old colleague, the 73-year-old Dr. Carl Gille (1813–99) whom Liszt called "my untiring friend of many years standing" (LLB, vol. 2, p. 253). Gille was a lawyer and chief magistrate at Jena. Years earlier he had established the custom of organizing an annual Liszt concert in Jena, whither Liszt and his pupils would journey from Weimar. Anna Spierling was one of their number, and this is where the recently widowed Gille may have met her. Gille was called upon to deliver a graveside oration at Liszt's funeral less than two weeks after this conversation took place.

himself, but he could have imparted [news of] this domestic change to me."[31]

Then Göllerich returned. He was unable to get any tickets before 12 noon. The Master asked him to read a chapter from Locke's work about music, his daughter having drawn attention to it that morning.[32] In the meantime, I told the Master a few things about Pest, about his coachman, etc., as well as the unhappy news about the king of Bavaria that had greatly distressed me. The Master said, "Distressed, distressed! Many things are distressing in life, but after all the things that he did, one didn't know what to think any more. The only thing which does not appear to make him insane was that he put an end to his own life. By the way, apropos of that event, my duke [Carl Alexander] has once again distinguished himself. Ten years ago in Weimar a little princess died and Bavaria took no notice of it. So he now felt compelled to omit sending an aide to the funeral of the king."[33]

31. By itself, this little bit of gossip about Gille and the young Anna Spierling hardly rises to the level of anecdote. But the psychological significance of the story is not lost on us, nor, we suspect, would it have been lost on Lina. Liszt was drawing an unconscious parallel between himself and Lina on the one hand and Gille and Anna on the other.

32. Liszt was no stranger to the writing of the English philosopher John Locke (1632–1704), whose works he had started to read as a young man in Paris, in the early 1830s. In a letter to his pupil Pierre Wolff (LLB, vol. 1, p. 7) he mentions Locke as one of several writers in whose work he was already absorbed. The particular work of Locke containing his ideas on music, and passed along to Liszt by Cosima, would have been his essay "Some Thoughts Concerning Education" (1693).

33. Liszt is referring to the suicide of King Ludwig II of Bavaria, on June 13, 1886, to whose funeral Grand Duke Carl Alexander had refused to send a representative. The "little princess" to whom Liszt refers, and whose death

I answered that I did not find this especially brilliant. The Master thought that this quality could not be praised in him at all, therefore he completely shared my point of view. "By the way, I don't think that Bavaria noticed this great loss. The ceremonies would have taken place even without Weimar."

The Master continued to talk a great deal. I remarked, somewhat inconsiderately, "Master, your hair has become thinner." The Master looked at me sadly and said, "So I have lost even that as well." I told the Master a good deal about Pest, also about the King, his coachman. Then Siloti,[34]

Ludwig had ignored, was the stillborn child of Princess Maria Anna, the daughter of Grand Duke Carl Alexander, who had presented the monarch with a dead granddaughter in January 1877. What had made the tragedy such a difficult burden for Carl Alexander to bear was that his eldest sister Princess Maria Louise Alexandria (1808–77) had died around the same time. The Weimar Court had been plunged into mourning for several weeks, with no sign of sympathy from King Ludwig.

King Ludwig had drowned himself in Lake Starnberg, as a result of a conspiracy against him by some of his high-ranking ministers. His doctor Bernhard von Gudden was drowned with him, attempting to save the King's life. Liszt had been informed of Ludwig's suicide by Carl Alexander as early as June 14, just a day after the tragedy occurred. Göllerich reports that Liszt came back after his meeting with the grand duke, silent and depressed, and suddenly blurted out, "That is a dreadful solution! The grand duke has just told me that the king has met his end in Lake Starnberg!" (GL, p. 176). Liszt was a great admirer of King Ludwig, especially for his support of Wagner. His oratorio *St. Elisabeth* is dedicated to the monarch. It is interesting to find Liszt telling Schmalhausen that Ludwig's suicide was a sign not of his insanity but of his intelligence. Many students of the topic have meanwhile concluded that the medical report on Ludwig, signed on June 10 by four doctors who never even examined him but had a vested interest in diagnosing him as "paranoid," was a thoroughly bogus document, a political instrument whose sole purpose was to unseat the king.

34. Alexander Siloti (1863–1945) had been a student of Liszt since 1883.

Stavenhagen, Thomán,[35] etc, arrived. The Master went into the salon with us and sat down again on the green sofa. Lessmann arrived as well, and La Janina became a topic of conversation. The Master said, "She was not bad, simply unbalanced. In my opinion she was decidedly talented. Is she resigning from the position in which she holds three posts?" Lessmann then read to the Master Janina's advertisement from his magazine.[36]

He had studied at the Moscow Conservatory under Nicholas Rubinstein for piano and Tchaikovsky for composition and had then settled in Leipzig where he met Liszt. Siloti joined the Weimar masterclass each summer while keeping Leipzig as his base of operations. In Leipzig Siloti had also founded, with Martin Krause, the first "Liszt Verein" devoted to the promotion of Liszt's music (much against Liszt's will, it has to be said). After Liszt's death Siloti moved back to Moscow where he taught the piano at the Moscow Conservatory. Among his first students was his cousin Sergei Rachmaninov. He also took up conducting, pioneering first performances in Russia of music by the young Stravinsky, Scriabin, Debussy, and Schoenberg. These activities were brought to a halt by the Russian revolution and he left Russia in 1919, settling with his family in New York, where he joined the piano faculty of The Juilliard School in 1924. See the photograph on p. 63.

35. István Thomán (1862–1940), a Hungarian pupil of Liszt, later had a distinguished teaching career at the Liszt Academy in Budapest. His pupils included Dohnányi and Bartók.

36. It is fascinating to find such generous observations coming from Liszt, since Olga Janina, the self-styled "Cossack Countess," had introduced much pain into his life in earlier years. She was not a Cossack, she was not a countess, and her name was not "Janina." She was born Olga Zielinski-Piasecka, into a lower-middle-class Polish family in Lvov. Her father had made money through patenting an improved kind of boot polish, and this gave her the independence to study the piano and to travel. "Janina" was the name of her first husband (who, according to her own account, she married when she was only seventeen and left after the wedding night), and she adopted it because it had a better "ring" to it. Olga was unstable and addicted to drugs. She met Liszt in Rome, in 1869, became his pupil, and im-

Göllerich had gone for my tickets and returned with them. As he handed them over, the Master said, "Let me see them. What do they look like? In which row are they?" Everyone regarded me with a condescending smile when it became apparent that the Master had bought the tickets for me. Soon the Master sent everybody away and said, "Lina and Göllerich I will keep here."

Göllerich went out for a few minutes, and I remained seated with the Master on the green sofa. The Master told me now why Frau Jaëll was angry with him. The end of this story was that she told the Master, "You only think about one

mediately set out to conquer him. Having been rebuffed by him and inflamed with jealousy, she pursued the composer to Hungary, and turned up at his Budapest apartment with a revolver, threatening to shoot him and then take poison. He disarmed her, but failed to prevent her from swallowing the "poison," which turned out to be harmless. Olga was given an ultimatum by Liszt's powerful Hungarian friends: either leave Budapest or face deportation by the police. She settled in Paris where she devoted the next several years to writing a series of autobiographical novels, which were designed to cause Liszt embarrassment. The best known was *Les Amours d'une Cosaque par un ami de l'Abbé 'X'"* (Paris, 1875), published under the pseudonym "Sylvia Zorelli," which purports to describe an intimate relationship with Liszt in 1869 and 1870. For a fuller account of Olga's checkered career, see WFL, vol. 3, pp. 171–90.

The magazine advertisement to which Liszt refers appeared in AMZ, which Lessmann edited, in its issue of 23/30 July 1886, p. 317. Olga there used her married name of Olga Cézano, having married Paul Cézano, a Russian émigré of private means, a few years earlier. In it she announced that from July 12 she was resigning her positions of "sa présidence, sa direction et son concours" at the Geneva Academy of Music, and that from September 1 she was opening a School for Advanced Piano Playing and Harmony. The language of the advertisement may have been inflated. Although she taught the piano at the Geneva Conservatory, she held no permanent administrative positions there.

woman!" Just as the Master finished relating it, Göllerich entered and caught these last few words.

[From the supplement dated July 23:] The story of Frau Jaëll was as follows. "As you know," Liszt confided, "Frau Jaëll had already written to me in Pest that she wanted to organize a Liszt concert for my reception in Paris. I requested her not to do that, but rather to organize a small gathering in her house. A few stations before we got to Paris, [Pauline] Viardot and a few other ladies drove out to join me, and I arrived with them in Paris. Frau Jaëll was at the station and was greatly offended to see me in this company. Frau Montigny had announced a Liszt concert without my knowledge, and I had no alternative but to attend. This meant that it was all over with Mme. Jaëll. She too gave a concert and of course I attended that one as well. She played well, and I went to compliment her afterward. But she vouchsafed no answer and said only, 'There is only one woman on your mind.' I asked her if she was referring to Fräulein Schmalhausen. Then I fell ill, lay in bed, and could not very well receive her at the Munkácsy's. This spoiled everything." (I asked if she was not popular with the Munkácsys. The Master replied, "Not especially.") "In brief, she did not put in an appearance again and did not say goodbye to me. I don't know what is the matter with people today."

Siegfried then arrived to pick up the Master for dinner. The Master led me into the bedroom and said, "Expect me this afternoon in the large concourse over the festival square in front of the main door. We will meet there." He kissed me and rejoined Siegfried in the salon and went with him to Wahnfried to dine. I went to the performance, waited in front of the main door, but in vain. The Master did not come. Schorn patrolled up and down with Dingeldey, following me with her fish eyes. Of course, she did not know for whom I was waiting for I felt physically unwell and very irritated. I could only drink a glass of beer at Vogel's that evening in Göllerich's company. And Göllerich took me home straight afterward.

Saturday, July 24

By 8:00 A.M. I was waiting in Miska's room. The Master had told me yesterday always to wait there until his daughter had left. By 8:30 A.M. Cosima had departed, and I greeted the Master in the bedroom. He apologized for yesterday afternoon, about not having come down [to meet me], but he had coughed so severely that he was not allowed to go. He told me that he had dined near the loge with Hatzfeldt, his nephew, etc., that he had eaten almost nothing, and that the children did not have enough to eat because everything was sold out in the large restaurant.

The Master then said, "Isn't it true, Lina? The day before yesterday you refused to play cards simply because Lessmann was playing. I have the pleasure of Lessmann's company, from four to six o'clock for a game of cards. Will you exclude yourself this afternoon as well?" I replied that I had really forgotten how to play cards. Lessmann I was less bothered about. In [Liszt's] house I would never provoke unpleasant situations, out of respect for him.

[From the supplement dated July 24:] During the game of

whist the Master often said "Miserable!" And: "We have made constant use of your misery, dear Lina."[37]

We now went into the salon, ever with Göllerich, of course. (I was surprised to see Göllerich with the Master so often. In Pest and Rome he only came during the lesson hours, and that was it.) The Master sat down in the large green armchair, Göllerich beside him and I on the other side on the sofa. Again Göllerich had to read something. I repeatedly gave the Master his water with wine. However, the Master constantly requested, "add only very little wine." I told the Master that the wine was the only thing left that would give him strength, that he ate nothing, and that the eternal drinking of water would only balloon his stomach. He said, "I am always so thirsty and I have been forbidden to drink wine." During the reading, the beloved Master often fell asleep, his head lowering itself onto the left shoulder. While the head was bowed he had an indescribably sweet, charitable smile. Whenever he raised his head, he sighed deeply, and his features became distorted as if in deep pain. Thus it continued, smiling one second, sighing the next, for an hour and a half. Then he woke up and looked around. Göllerich and I were sitting beside him as before. He immediately regained his sunny smile and indicated for Göllerich to continue, that he was listening. But soon he again fell into this dream-slumber.

37. Having forgotten, or never learned, how to play whist, Lina was nonetheless frequently recruited by Liszt to make up a foursome—often with lamentable results.

The princess of Meiningen[38] then arrived with her gentle-man- and lady-in-waiting; a few minutes earlier Frau Blume, Stavenhagen, Siloti, etc. had shown up. The Master asked me to play something, but I had not looked at a piano for weeks and declined. He asked who was standing closest to the piano. Stavenhagen stood there but immediately ducked behind a large chair. The Master noticed this maneuver and said, "That won't help you, Stavenhagen: go to the piano, right now." Everyone laughed, including the Master. Staven-hagen now had to sit down, and he played the 3rd *Liebe-straum* ["O lieb"].[39] More and more people continued to arrive, and because there was not enough room in the salon, I went into the bedroom with Frau Blume and Fräulein Lüder. The Master followed us and asked, "Lina, do you know where my coat is?" He had his velvet jacket on and wanted to put on his coat for the Princess. Miska was not present and he was used to the idea of my helping him. I now took off his velvet jacket and helped him put on the coat, combed his hair quickly, and he went back into the salon.

38. Marie-Elisabeth, princess of Meiningen (1853–1923), was a regular supporter of the Bayreuth Festival, but this had not prevented Wagner from being highly critical of her glacial personality. Cosima reports that when she asked Wagner how such an aloof personality might be reborn, Wagner had replied, "As a spittoon" (WT, vol. 2, p. 505).

39. This observation removes a question mark from the Liszt literature: there *was* a piano in Liszt's lodgings in Bayreuth. Whether he himself touched the keyboard during these difficult days, however, is not known. But for those scholars with a keen interest in determining the exact moment when the fingers of "the king of pianists" fell silent, the Bayreuth trip pro-vides a possible alternative to the "farewell" concert he had given in Lux-embourg on July 19.

Frau Blume seemed to find that my actions of dressing the Master in his coat were not proper, for she cast a meaningful glance toward Göllerich and Fräulein Lüder. After Stavenhagen's playing, all the people soon took their leave and I remained with Göllerich and the Master. The Master was not especially friendly toward Göllerich, who read something to him. Then I told the Master that we wanted to leave and that he should sleep a little as the talking had strained him a lot. He said, "All right, but return in time for the card game this afternoon." Then he abruptly dismissed Göllerich. I now bent over him and kissed his forehead and hand. The Master believed Göllerich had gone out. He drew me onto his knee, pressed me tightly to himself, put my head beside his, and said, "My dear, dear, good Lina," and gazed at me terribly sadly. The Master looked so tired and unhappy that I did not want him to see the tears in my eyes from the pain, and I fled so that I could have a good cry. Göllerich was indiscreet enough to remain standing at the door, even though he had been dismissed, and he now came up to me and said, "Aren't you pleased that you can be away from the Master for the longest time, and yet he receives you with equal warmth on every occasion?" In fact, I went home with a happy but fearful feeling; I felt that the Master cared for me deeply, and this weighed a *thousand times* more than *all* the thorns and pinpricks. I returned home feeling very ill and lay down on the sofa for a few hours without eating anything.

In the afternoon, around four o'clock, I returned to the Master who looked very weak and frail. He sat on a pile of

Franz Liszt in the circle of his pupils on his seventy-third birthday, Weimar, October 22, 1884. Front row from left: Saul Liebling, Alexander Siloti, Arthur Friedheim, Emil von Sauer, Alfred Reisenauer, and Alexander Gottschalg. Back row from left: Moriz Rosenthal, Viktoria Drewing, Mele Paramanoff, Franz Liszt, Friedheim's mother, and Hugo Mansfeldt. Photograph by Louis Held.

pillows on the green sofa, with me beside him, playing cards with Göllerich, Stavenhagen, Thomán, and Siloti. Later came Lassen.[40] Yesterday's performance was discussed. Lessmann said that it was truly exemplary. The Master replied,

40. Eduard Lassen (1830–1904) was a composer and conductor and a

"But consider, dear friend, it goes without saying that after having rehearsed it for so many years, and performed and played it together, the singers and the orchestra can do it in their sleep."

> [From the supplement dated July 24:] The Master said to Thomán, "Haynald[41] has asked about you. He liked your 'Rossignol' very much." To Stavenhagen he said, "Is it not true, Stavenhagen, that the Cardinal demanded this piece from you as well, but you had not studied it?"[42]

Lessmann now mentioned Bülow's genius with regard to turning names around. I said that, with due respect to Bülow, I did not find his practice of twisting names witty. The Master said, "No, I also am not a friend of twisting names around; that is cheap."[43]

---

close disciple of Liszt, who had helped his career in earlier years by (among other things) staging and conducting Lassen's opera *Landgraf Ludwig's Brautfahrt* in Weimar (1857) after it had been turned down elsewhere. In 1858 Lassen had succeeded Liszt as Court Music Director in Weimar. Two of Liszt's finest song transcriptions are of Lassen's "Ich weil' in tiefer Einsamkeit" and "Löse, Himmel, meine Seele."

41. Cardinal Lajos Haynald (1816–91) was an old friend of Liszt and was now the primate of Hungary. It was Haynald who had chaired the national committee overseeing the arrangements for the celebration of the Liszt Jubilee in 1873. Liszt had recently met Haynald at Colpach Castle, just before coming to Bayreuth, where the primate had broken his journey en route to Brussels for an audience with Leopold II, king of the Belgians.

42. "Le Rossignol" (The Nightingale) is based on a song by the Russian composer Alabieff. It dates from 1842, the time of Liszt's first visit to Russia.

43. Bülow was notorious for his sarcasm, his biting wit, and his ability to create puns at the expense of friend and foe alike. He once ran into the

The Master requested a few gumdrops, which Göllerich got for him. I had to scrape the sugar from them, after which he ate them. The Master then asked me to pass the Marsala around. I had a headache and did not pour any for myself. The Master pushed a glass of wine toward me and said, "At least try a little, dear Lina." Because the Master began to find it difficult to hold the cards, much less to order them, I always placed them in his hands in the right sequence. Fraülein von Schorn now arrived. I wanted to give her my place on the sofa, but the Master held me down with his left hand and said, "Do not move from my side, dear Lina, I am not fond of changes." Later he asked me to play [cards] with him at least once; this I did, but I saw how his eyes were drooping with fatigue and said, "Master, why don't you let

---

young American violinist and Liszt-follower Arma Senkrah, who had de-rived her unusual name by running most of her real one backwards: Mary Harkness. Undaunted by the cut and thrust of Bülow's conversation, Ms. Senkrah had the temerity to show him one of her recent newspaper reviews, beneath which Bülow wrote "Bravo!" When she pointed out to him that his approval was meaningless unless he signed it, Bülow picked up his pen and wrote beneath it: "Snah nov Wolüb." The bewildered Senkrah pressed Bülow to explain his strange signature, whereupon he informed her that he was merely following her own example. See the amusing wordplay on Lina Schmalhausen's own name, by Xaver Scharwenka, page 7.

Despite Liszt's protestations about Bülow, he himself in earlier years had frequently indulged in witty name twisting. The younger of his two pupils named Grosskurth he had dubbed "Kleinkurth." Another pupil Fräulein Häuptling had her name rendered by him into English as Miss Chief, or "mischief." Yet another student, Henryk van Zeyl from Amsterdam, was re-ferred to as "the Flying Dutchman." This practice reached the height of ab-surdity with Annette Essipoff, a pupil (and later the wife) of the great pedagogue Leschetizky, whom he called the "Essig-topf," or "vinegar bottle."

Stavenhagen hold your cards?" (The younger people just had no talent for reading things from Liszt's eyes.) The Master agreed, and I played with Stavenhagen. In this manner, the Master looked over Stavenhagen's shoulder for a moment before falling into a heavy slumber. Lassen asked me to stop because Schorn was making signs to him that when the Master opened his eyes, the match could be said to be over. Schorn said, "Dear Master, I think it is better that we leave you now, for you must have some rest." The Master answered, "Yes, I will attempt to sleep a little. Dear Lina, you stay with me, since you never disturb me. Göllerich can stay as well and read something aloud."

[From the supplement dated July 24:] Around seven o'-clock in the evening, when the Master was sitting in the bedroom with Göllerich and myself, Mihalovich[44] arrived. The Master was very fatigued, and Miska chattered constantly without any regard for him. Mihalovich said that Erkel had compromised himself in Pest, etc. The Master asked me to show Mihal[ovich] his picture (a photograph of Munkácsy's portrait). I said that I found it horrible.[45] The Master then said [in defense of the artist Munkácsy], "No, no, Lina. I don't like it when my friends are abused. By the way, Lina will have to take a picture of me soon."

44. The Hungarian composer Ödön Mihalovich (1842–1929) was one of Liszt's most trusted Hungarian colleagues. He had played a leading role in having the troublesome Olga Janina evicted from Budapest after she had threatened Liszt's life. He was later to take over Liszt's position as president of the Royal Hungarian Academy of Music.

45. This famous portrait of Liszt in old age, which not everyone in Liszt's circle admired, is reproduced as the frontispiece to this book.

Siloti asked the Master whether tomorrow morning he could speak with him alone for a moment. The Master asked him to come at 8:00 A.M. For a while, the Master stayed with us in the salon, until Siegfried came to escort him to Wahnfried. From there he went to the Hatzfeldts for a game of whist with his nieces.

The Master coughed and rattled terribly. All he continued to drink was water. Earlier Siloti had brought him a new kind of cigar and had given them the name "Liszt Society Cigars" (the Liszt Society sells them). The Master said that for the time being he could not smoke, but that as soon as he recovered this would be the first cigar he would try.

He then told Göllerich and me that his eyes were failing to serve him, that he was almost blind. "This I probably deserved, but the dropsy I did not deserve at all."[46] Again he looked so gloomy when he said that.

46. Much on Liszt's mind at this time was the prospect of an operation for the removal of a cataract on the left eye, scheduled to take place in Halle, in September of this year.

Sunday, July 25

Early around 8:00 A.M. I went to the Master, but I had to wait for an eternity because of Cosima, whose coffee arrived late from Wahnfried. When Cosima left, Göllerich was still not there, so I went in search of the Master in the salon. He sat in his green armchair sleeping soundly. After the conversation with Cosima he seemed to be *very* fatigued. Again he gave me his hand and asked if Göllerich was there, and that he wanted to try to sleep a little, and just to sit down, that I didn't disturb him. Soon Göllerich returned, and the Master asked him to read again, this time from Wagner's writings. The Master felt very poorly and said that the many conversations with various people were exhausting, and that he wanted to see *no one,* with the exception of Frau Menter who was arriving today, Frau Blume who was leaving today, and Mme Tardieu[47]—*no one* else, whoever it might be unless, perhaps, Stavenhagen for a few moments, but only if it

47. Malwine Tardieu (d. 1896) was married to Charles Tardieu, the editor of the Brussels newspaper *L'Indépendance Belge.* She kept Liszt informed of all things musical happening in Brussels, including performances of his own music. Liszt had stayed as a guest of Malwine and Charles Tardieu when he visited Brussels in May 1882 for the first performance in French of his oratorio *Saint Elisabeth.* He had also seen them again in the spring of 1886.

were absolutely necessary. The Master repeated all this to Miska who left grumbling and said, "Your Grace, I will let no one in; what do these people want with Your Grace anyway, when Your Grace is ill?" This angered the Master greatly, and he said in a very agitated tone that I should go right away and tell Miska that if he does not let in the persons just named, he would receive a sound blow—and to tell him this very firmly since the fellow has a thick skull, and this is none of his business. I went to Miska and gave him the Master's orders. Miska replied that Stavenhagen would not get in as long as the Master was sick, that by rights only he [Miska] and I should be near him. When I returned to the Master he asked, "Did you tell him firmly? Otherwise he will really receive a blow."[48] Then I sat down on the left of the Master, he in the armchair, I on the sofa. Göllerich was on the right and read aloud.

[From the supplement dated July 25:] The Master sat in the salon with me and Göllerich. He told me that Varga[49] had

48. The thought of Liszt threatening to beat his servant, still less the spectacle of him actually doing so, beggars the imagination. Doubtless such things happened often enough between master and servant in the nineteenth century; but if Liszt's relations with his various valets and manservants (all of whom are well documented) across the years tell us anything at all about him, it is that he treated such people with kindness, and was invariably trusting and solicitous toward them. This threat of aggression attributed to Liszt by Schmalhausen, if true, is much more indicative of the increasing isolation and helplessness he was experiencing during his final days than of any hostility he might have felt toward Miska.

49. Dr. Ferenc Varga (1835–98) was a Hungarian physician to the Franciscans, and Liszt was a welcome guest in his home whenever he visited Budapest. His daughter Vilma (1865–1950) was a gifted pianist who had been

written to him and had inquired about his health. He had returned a few lines through Göllerich with the comment that he would not tolerate any inquiries about his health. The Master told me that he hardly wrote letters anymore. "Those [I send] to you belong to the few exceptions that I still manage to write," he said significantly. During the mid-day meal the Master pointed to Belli and said, "Does he have something to eat as well? Miska, give him something." And to me, "Now that you have acquired him, you should care for him as well. I think that he will only disturb you when you practice."

I explained to the Master that I had often encountered Frau Árkövy.[50] "Yes," he replied, "She was always terribly nervous. There was nothing to be done about her piano playing."

It was not long before Miska came and announced the arrival of the Master's relatives from Vienna (the wife of the imperial prosecutor and her two children).[51] Liszt made

---

Liszt's pupil at the Royal Academy of Music in Hungary since 1884. Liszt's highly characteristic comment that he would not tolerate any inquiries about his health takes on the trappings of wry humor once we understand that the message was directed toward a medical doctor.

50. Katalin Árkövy, the wife of Professor József Árkövy (1851–1922), Liszt's Hungarian dentist.

51. Henrietta Liszt (1825–1920) was actually the widow of Liszt's uncle, Eduard Liszt (1817–79), who had occupied the highest legal position in the Austro-Hungarian Empire, namely the office of royal and imperial public prosecutor. After Eduard's death in 1879, Liszt had kept in regular touch with these Viennese relatives. The two "children" accompanying Henrietta were the twenty-year-old Hedwig (1866–1941) and the nineteen-year-old Eduard (1867–1961).

an impatient gesture, saying, "Oh, the princess sends her to me again; I don't care, let them enter." The Master remained seated and hardly greeted them (he was so exhausted); he asked them to sit down and said nothing for a long time. Then he turned slightly to the right and said to the young son, "Good day, Eduard, I have not greeted you yet." The latter kissed his hand and told him that his brother had matriculated at Marburg [University] and that he was now visiting him there. The Master said to the young woman that he had not been aware that she was a vocal artist, but that "one of my young friends in Weimar told me this." "Surely you read in the musical press that I sing in the choir," she said, supplemented immediately by a remark from the imperial prosecutor's wife, namely, that Eduard also sings in the choir. The conversation became very insipid, and the Master fell into a leaden slumber. His relatives then spoke a lot with Göllerich. Frau Liszt uttered a big speech about the depravity and falseness of people and yelled so loudly that I feared the Master would awake at any moment. After an hour and a half the Master opened his eyes, and the imperial prosecutor's wife said, "You have just had a healthy and good sleep." The Master said, "I feel horribly weary." The relatives soon took their leave, and the Master asked Göllerich to continue to read aloud. Göllerich excused himself and said that he had to leave to pick up his sister from the railway station; she was arriving here for today's performance. I continued to read in Göllerich's place.

Shortly afterward the doctor was announced.[52] The Master said, "Stay, dear Lina." But Miska whispered to me to go into the bedroom for a few moments. This I did; the doctor then spoke briefly with the Master, and when Liszt asked him, "Can I go to the performance tonight?" he replied, "Certainly you can go, but take care not to speak so much, because this taxes the lungs. It would be better not to receive so many visitors." The Master asked, "Should I have my small meal brought here and not go over to Wahnfried?" The doctor said, "Yes, that would be better." Then he had Miska show him the chamber pot and said, "Oh, it is considerably better than before; the urine is much lighter and in a few days you will have overcome this little cold." I now looked at the pot in the bedroom. I thought I saw *ink* and was alarmed. Miska said, "Oh, that means nothing, it has been like that for three weeks already."[53]

I caught up with the doctor in the hallway and asked him to tell me honestly how the Master's condition was. He stroked me under the chin and said, "Dear child, so far there is nothing to worry about. He should not speak so much and receive too many people, otherwise it could develop into pneumonia. But don't be afraid, dear child; for the time being there is no danger at all. Just make sure that he gets a

52. This was the Wagners' family physician, Dr. Karl Landgraf, who had been summoned at Cosima's request.

53. The symptom suggests that Liszt was passing blood through the urine. If, as Miska observed, the urine had been contaminated for three weeks, Liszt was evidently already seriously ill at Colpach.

bowl of pure broth every day and abstains from drinking wine." The doctor left, and I had a distasteful feeling about him; he seemed to me to be an unscrupulous old dandy who did not understand the Master's illness. When I returned to the Master in the salon, he said, "Lina, I am approaching my end. The doctor doesn't understand me. I have no confidence in him. He always says it's already going better. My God, then I should feel cured already, but I feel that every day I am getting worse." The Master was infinitely sad and said this with a low voice in broken sentences. Speaking put a strain on him, and his eyes were always half closed. I told him, "Dear Master, above all you should not receive any visitors. The doctor just told me that if you do not look after yourself, pneumonia could develop." The Master said dully, "I thought that I had already had it for a long time." I then went to Miska to tell him that he should fetch something for dinner from over there. From now on a bowl of broth should be sent across to the Master every day. Miska told me, "You haven't said anything to the old man about pneumonia? It's already bad enough to get along with him. He thinks that he is half dead already, and if he should hear that, it will be all over with him." I let the stupid fellow prattle on and again told him to fetch the food. Miska came to the Master in the salon. Liszt said, "Go down and say that I am not feeling well enough to go over there. I want to spare myself for today's performance, and the little that I eat should be sent across to me." Miska then brought him some smoked veal cutlet with apricot sauce. The Master ate almost nothing, only a little of the sauce with which he drank water. He poured me a glass of wine, and with it I received as usual his "house mon-key"[54] (a favorite term of his when we were alone), my bis-cuit and sauce. The Master pointed to little Belli and said, "Did he get anything? Since you have acquired him you have to take care of him as well. Miska, give him the meat from my plate." The Master coughed so severely that it was im-possible for him to utter complete sentences without stop-ping in between, his face always becoming bloodred. The Master said, "It is a nuisance that I had to choose Bayreuth of all places to become sick, to set myself right under the noses of those people, it is really too awkward."

Frau Menter now arrived, accompanied by Dingeldey and her counselor Jett.[55] The Master was not especially friendly toward her (perhaps his indifference was due to his illness). She looked delightful in a light-red silk dress, rich with lace, bare neck and arms, and wearing a delightful light-red satin

54. "Hausaffe." This is possibly a term of endearment for Lina receiving tidbits as a reward for domestic services.

55. Liszt regarded Sophie Menter (1846–1918) as his most gifted female piano student. The daughter of Joseph Menter, the cellist, Sophie had been a child prodigy and was already touring Germany by the age of fifteen. In 1867, she became a pupil of Carl Tausig in Berlin. Two years later she joined Liszt's masterclasses in Weimar and remained with him for several years. In 1872 she married the cellist David Popper, from whom she was divorced in 1886. At the time of this last encounter with Liszt, Menter was a professor at the St. Petersburg Conservatory of Music (1883–87). She was also the com-poser of a number of charming salon pieces. Tchaikovsky, whom she got to know during her Russian sojourn, orchestrated her *Ungarische Zigeuner-weisen* for piano and orchestra, and she performed it under his direction in Odessa, on February 4, 1893. From comments Schmalhausen makes a bit later in the narrative, we gather that Herr Jett may have been Menter's le-gal adviser. She was at that moment in the midst of her divorce proceedings.

hat. The hat and neck were decorated with the loveliest white colors. Frau Menter took a seat on a chair by the Master's right side; I sat at the Master's left. The Master took hold of a piece of the edge of the lace of Frau Menter's dress and said to me, "Lina, isn't that a pretty lace?" The Master asked Menter who her newest worshipper was. Frau Menter replied that she had never had any other than this one (pointing to her parasol with a wood carving of a cat on the handle).[56] The Master said, "You announced yourself for 11:00 A.M. this morning, but at that time you were probably still in bed. Well, that's your right, for whoever employs her remaining time as you do can allow herself that."

Frau Menter now told us a few things about Madame Cézano,[57] that she encouraged her students to be just as crazy as she is; and that she [Menter] found it incomprehensible that Bülow was so delighted with Madame Cézano as a pianist. Bülow had recently assured her that she played the last sonatas of Beethoven masterfully. Liszt inquired how long she [Menter] intended to stay, and she replied only for the performance this afternoon. The Master thought that this was too short a visit. Sophie replied, "Dear Master, I

56. Sophie Menter was famous for her love of felines, several of which had a free run of Itter Castle, her home in the Austrian Tyrol.

57. See n. 36 for more information about Madame Cézano, alias Olga Janina. Sophie Menter's remarks about the high opinion in which Olga's Beethoven playing was held by Hans von Bülow are confirmed by the *Allgemeine Musik-Zeitung*. Evidently she had accompanied von Bülow a few days earlier when he had played at a concert arranged by Professor Eschmann for the students of the Lausanne Conservatory of Music. She is described there as "the excellent professor of piano playing from the Geneva Conservatory" (AMZ, July 9/16, 1886, p. 292).

would have considered staying longer, but when I saw Dingeldey standing at the train station, I wanted to turn around right away." The Master said, "Well then, let us see to it that Dingeldey leaves." The Master asked Menter to hand him a couple of [playing] cards and return again tomorrow, and she took her leave of him. When she had gone we spoke about Dingeldey. The Master said, "He is an importunate babbler who immediately brags about each acquaintance. Well, Sophie gave him a piece of her mind." I said that [Dingeldey] was now wearing handsome gold things (a watch, a necklace, rings, etc.) and a pretty velvet jacket; whereas before he used to walk around in things that were frayed. Liszt said, "That is the best sign that he has little in his pocket. Such people have to impress from the outside."

Earlier, as the Master was conversing with Frau Menter and the others, he had in his hand a handkerchief in a dreadful condition because of the frequent bringing up of phlegm. All eyes were glued to it, but the Master did not notice it at all and continued to use the handkerchief. I went into the bedroom to the linen chest and brought him a clean handkerchief; the old one I removed. The Master looked at me with such a thankful glance and said, "Oh, Lina, you are already just as at home here as you were in Pest." I asked the Master, weary from all the talking, to rest for a while, and he said, "Good, I will try to sleep, leave me alone for a while."

I then went home and got ready for today's performance. In the theater I constantly had to look around at the beloved Master. He sat beside Princess [Marie von] Hatzfeldt in the loge. In spite of the deep darkness during the performance

I could always find his head, his "Godlike mane" being my most reliable light. Understandably, my attention was very divided because I knew the Master to be ill. Consequently I looked more toward his loge than the stage. I noticed every movement of the head by the position of the hair. In the entr'acte the Master remained seated in the loge with [Princess] Hatzfeldt speaking eternally into his ears. He then had to answer her through an ear trumpet, as the good woman is almost deaf (most merciful, I thought, for the Master).

At the end of *Tristan* the artists received jubilant ovations.[58] The Master's dear hands were applauding along with the others, and even when everyone else had stopped I saw his hands (on the right a black silk glove) still beating together to encourage people to applaud further. I don't know what moved me so much, perhaps the performance. I went home with Göllerich and his sister and wept the whole way. Having reached home, I went to bed without dinner but could not fall asleep for a long time and started to cry again.

58. Although the diary does not mention it, this performance of Wagner's *Tristan*, on Sunday, July 25, was the first time that the opera had ever been performed in Bayreuth, and Cosima regarded her father's attendance in the opera house as a mandatory aspect of public relations. Liszt knew it and responded accordingly. He once described himself ironically as "Bayreuth's poodle."

Monday, July 26

I arrived at the Master's early, at 8:00 A.M. He sat sleeping on the green chair in the salon. I awakened him and said that Göllerich was ill and in bed and had asked to be excused. The Master said, "The poor fellow, he should be told from me not to get up too early and to take care of himself." The Master asked me to read something to him. I read the French papers, which Munkácsy had sent him. They dealt with the Master and his best student Stavenhagen (at least, that's how the newspaper put it). Then I had to read him that rubbish [*Kram*] by Wagner; and from Lessmann's *Musik-Zeitung* I had to read Mottl's biography.[59] The Master often fell asleep, but I continued to read, since he did not seem to like it when he was caught sleeping. I pretended that I didn't notice and went on reading yet more blather [*Stiefel*].

59. Felix Mottl (1856–1911) was the chief conductor of the Karlsruhe Philharmonic Society where in a few short years he had raised the standards of orchestral playing to a national level. He had been associated with the Bayreuth Festival since 1876 and was now jointly in charge of the present productions of *Tristan* and *Parsifal*. Lina could hardly have enjoyed reading the article on Mottl to Liszt. This was the same Mottl who had accompanied her disastrous performance of Liszt's A major Concerto in Karlsruhe two years earlier, which had brought her some public notoriety (see p. 5.).

When the Master awoke, we both looked at the illustrations of the Bayreuth Festival brochure; whatever he could not see clearly I had to explain to him.

> [From the supplement dated July 26:] Early on, the Master asked me if I was going up [to the theater] tonight. I said no, but I would like to see *Tristan* once again. I told him that Göllerich was ill and could therefore not use his ticket for today. The Master said that perhaps he could still exchange it at the box office for another one, providing he sent it early in the morning. I asked the Master if he wanted to go to Russia this year and he replied, "Hardly. In the spring I would have gone, but my trip would have had no purpose because the grand duke would not have been there at that time."

Mme Tardieu from Brussels now arrived to take her leave. She asked the Master, "How are you?" The Master, who cannot stand this question, stuck out his tongue at her (which was red, like a cherry) and said, "You see my stomach is in the best condition." The Master also said to Tardieu, "Fräulein Schmalhausen was also in Aachen. I learned this only recently when I took a trip there."[60] And turning to me he added: "You never told me that, dear Lina. I believe that you have relatives there?" Mme Tardieu then told him that she would return in one week in the company of her husband,

60. Liszt is referring to his trip to Aachen, in June 1885, to attend a concert of his own music under the direction of the conductor Julius Kniese, where he had been reunited with the Tardieu family. Evidently Lina had been there without telling Liszt, another symptom of her anxiety to remain incognito whenever they were away from Budapest.

and that they both wanted to look up the Master, etc., etc. After endless idle chatter, she took her leave to make room for the visit of Liszt's relatives who had also come to say goodbye. The Master asked Hedwig to read him the last letter of the princess [Wittgenstein] but I first had to search for it everywhere because Miska had misplaced it. Later I went out to leave the relatives alone with the Master, but the Master came to fetch me and asked me to remain in the salon as his relatives would be leaving soon. The wife of the imperial prosecutor said, "We hope to see you soon in Vienna. We hope you will soon move into your little '*Kousinzimmer*' again."[61]

When they had left I had to tell the Master several things from Pest. I informed him that the day he had left, 20 pairs of silver knives and forks had been lost.[62] Mme Fábry suspected Miska, who, little by little, may have been providing for his dowry. The Master asked me, "To whom is the fellow engaged?" I said to the daughter of the coachman Mende in Weimar. The Master said, "Such things should never happen when I entrust Frau von Fábry with the supervision.[63] But

61. The "*Kousinzimmer*" was the family's name for the room that Liszt traditionally used whenever he visited Vienna and stayed with his relatives.

62. Liszt had left Budapest on March 11. But since, he had been traveling almost continuously, including making lengthy journeys to Paris, London, and Luxembourg before coming to Bayreuth. Lina had had no chance to impart news of the theft of knives and forks to him, which she evidently thought it better to disclose verbally. In light of the earlier thefts in Weimar, we can understand why she waited for five days before broaching such a sensitive topic: the right moment had only now presented itself.

63. Liszt had always occupied a private suite of rooms at the Royal Academy of Music in Budapest, the only "salary" he ever received for his services as president. For several years, Frau Amalie von Fábry had made this apart-

whom do you want me to hire in order to avoid this evil? My cousin from the country is useless for this job."

[From the supplement dated July 26:] The Master had two water pitchers (the color of the porcelain appeared different). Miska said that they were the same kind, but the Master did not trust him and said to me, "Lina, tell me what is written on this, and what on that one?" The Master spoke early with Joukowsky about Frau von Meyendorff and the apartment that ought to be rented for her. He wanted to know if she could not move into my apartment because I would already be leaving on the 1st. Joukowsky said, "I'll find an apartment." "As you please," said the Master. "The apartment of Fräulein Schmalhausen would not be bad. Don't forget to take a small adjoining room for Dorothea (the maid). So you will rent the apartment as of August 1st. The baroness will arrive here on the 2nd or 3rd, by the way. Read me her letter, dear friend," adding (because his relatives and I were there), "Please leave me alone for a few moments with Joukowsky. I have to speak to him." Joukowsky then read [Meyendorff's] letter to him.

Frau Menter now arrived. She was wearing some delightfully sweet lilac. I wanted to leave so she could be alone for a few moments with the Master; she would have none of it; nevertheless, I still left. She soon came after me. Outside Herr Jett was talking with Miska. I told the Master that Jett

---

ment secure from curiosity seekers and had taken care of his private possessions whenever he was abroad. In a letter to her, dated May 27, 1886, Liszt had instructed her, "I wish my rooms in Budapest to remain closed during my absence" (LLB, vol. 2, p. 391).

was outside, and the Master asked me to bring him in. Frau Menter behaved delightfully toward the Master. She always remained the grateful student. This moved me pleasantly, because the Master's present students speak to him *without respect and insolently*. Behind his back Stavenhagen, Thomán, etc., never say anything except "The old man is drunk; the old man is crazy." And such people Liszt, with his magnificent heart, introduces to the world and smooths their paths. The Master and Sophie by no means speak with praise about Friedheim and Dingeldey. About Friedheim the Master says, "Too bad about the talent, he is a completely miserable scoundrel." Sophie says, "Well, he is the most depraved creature that I can imagine; at least Dingeldey isn't quite that bad." The Master said, "In a different way, he is a scoundrel as well. Did he not carouse at your place in Itter last summer for six weeks without having been invited by you?" Sophie responded, "Granted, I was very surprised to have to count him among my guests at Itter." It continued in this way for a long time about her two erstwhile friends, Friedheim and Dingeldey.[64]

64. These highly damaging comments about Arthur Friedheim, who later became known in America as one of the most loyal of Liszt's disciples and a pioneering interpreter of his music, remind us once again that the circle of young people by whom he was now surrounded contained some individuals whose boisterous conduct had already drawn censure in Weimar and elsewhere. Even so, the words that Schmalhausen puts into Liszt's mouth are severe and out of character. One is left to wonder whether there might not be some special context that was omitted from her narrative. The rank hostility she felt toward Friedheim and Stavenhagen, especially, colors her view of them, as well as of the events in which these two young men were directly involved.

Sophie Menter. Photograph by J. Löwy, Vienna, 1873.

The Master then said, "I harmed myself greatly by the last trip to Luxembourg. Even there I had a severe cold for a week, and during the night Stavenhagen and Miska let me sit beside the open window of the railway carriage. They thought that the window could not be shut, and so I caught a cold. Sophie said that she would most likely never invite them to Itter again, after the reproaches which the baroness [Meyendorff] had made to her: namely, that she had had them with her for a few hours last October, and that she would never permit them to visit her again."

Menter and Jett now took their leave, and I again remained alone with the Master. Menter told me, "Take good care of the Master."

[From the supplement dated July 26:] Jett had commented to me that in the final scene of *Tristan,* the hidden orchestra was very disadvantageous. The Master asked, "Who made this brilliant statement?" I repeated "Jett." "Well," said Liszt, "I did not think that he was capable of such a stupid remark."

I told the Master that Jett did not seem to be a Christian. "That doesn't matter," the Master said, "I like him very much." I commented that Menter had again looked so pretty. The Master said, "It is unnatural. She is no longer in her youthful years. It is superb Parisian makeup." To my surprise, he did not utter a single word of praise about Menter.[65]

Göllerich had asked me this morning to try to persuade the Master to take him along to Bad Kissingen,[66] and even though the Master had already decided on Stradal for Kissin-

65. Was this because of Menter's forthcoming action for divorce? As a Catholic, Liszt disapproved of divorce as a means of terminating a marriage, as his critical stand against Cosima's own divorce from Hans von Bülow had made clear. It was Cosima's divorce and her subsequent remarriage to Richard Wagner in a Protestant church that had soured relations with her father for five years, from 1867 to 1872. Liszt condemned Cosima, and, in a chilling letter to her, withdrew his blessing from her (WFL, vol. 3, pp. 134–36).

66. For the water cure prior to the cataract operation.

gen, I should try to see that the Master took him along
instead. Admittedly he had no money, but the Master had
supported him so graciously in Weimar that he would likely
do so again in Kissingen. I now remembered Göllerich's request and began a conversation about the Master's impend-
ing trip to the spa. I said, "Dear Master, are you taking
Stradal along to Kissingen?" "Yes," he replied, "regrettably I
have no one who is better. I would have preferred Ramann[67]
and that would have worked quite well, but this again is not
possible because of the baroness [Meyendorff]; in the second place [Ramann] is ill herself and needs care. Peterle
[Meyendorff's eldest son, Peter] was initially to have accompanied me to Kissingen, but his job in Petersburg does
not permit it." I asked him, "Don't you want to take Göllerich

67. Lina Ramann (1833–1912) was Liszt's official biographer and was the
coprincipal (along with Ida Volckmann) of a flourishing school of music in
Nuremberg. The first volume of her life of Liszt had been published in 1881.
The second volume was still in preparation and would not appear until
1887, a year after Liszt's death. It was for Lina Ramann, of course, that
Schmalhausen wrote the present narrative, and we now understand why. Ramann's illness had not only prevented her from attending the Bayreuth Festival but also from traveling to the city for Liszt's funeral, so she lacked any
firsthand knowledge of the last few days of his life. Liszt's preference for
Ramann to accompany him to Kissingen is highly revealing—as is Liszt's
comment that Baroness Meyendorff would not have permitted it. The fact
is, he had absolutely no reason to suppose that he would die in Bayreuth.
But the water treatment in Kissingen, followed by the traumatic prospect of
eye surgery in Halle, already weighed on his mind, for he knew that there
was a chance he might lose his sight, perhaps worse. Ramann was someone
to whom he had for years entrusted many intimate details of his life. He was
still giving her interviews and answering her many questionnaires as late as
the summer of 1886, and this process would certainly have continued in
Kissingen and Halle had she been fit enough to accompany him there.

along?" He replied, "The poor fellow doesn't have a penny, and I am not wealthy enough to pay for his expenses. Stradal will probably get there during the next few days and arrange the accommodations. Frau von Meyendorff will come here to pick me up and will install me there and then perhaps leave Kissingen after a week." I said in that case I would come to him myself. The Master replied, "Yes, when she leaves, but perhaps she will have the idea of staying with me for the whole time. I will write you about this later." He continued, "I have planned everything until October, then I don't know where I will go. From here to Kissingen for three weeks; then from August until mid September to Halle, because of the operation; and then in October to Leipzig. But at the end of July I will still most certainly attend the musical concerts in Mainz, because I promised it." The Master now said, "Stay, dear Lina, and share my dinner with me." Miska brought the food (the doctor had ordered a broth for the midday meal, but the reply came from Wahnfried that broth would only be served twice a week). So the Master received no soup; just half an (over-cooked) chicken and an apple compote. The Master even wanted to share that wretched half chicken. I already balked at the thought because I observed the Master's increasing weakness and could not eat anything. But the Master thought that once again I did not like the food and said, "As long as one is not ill and as healthy as you are, one must eat; you are carrying on very foolishly and behaving badly." I now had to eat the rice with him from the same plate and with the same fork. The Master asked me if I was going to the theater today, and when I responded negatively

he said, "I can't go, I feel ill. Stay on the lookout this afternoon until those 'over there' have set out for the theater,
and then come to me immediately, for otherwise I will be
completely by myself and lonely." The Master frequently
touched the lower teeth on his right side, and I asked him if
he was in pain. "Not much," he said. "When I was young I
suffered greatly with my teeth."[68]

Suddenly the Master stared at the corner of the room far-
thest away and raised his voice, "That disgusting filth. That's
why I can't stand animals; they are all so dirty." I got quite a
shock. Belli had done something very naughty. I carried him
into the adjoining room and whacked him soundly. The
Master sat in the big green chair, faintly turned his head
around, and looked at the dog so compassionately, as if he
himself had felt every blow. So I stopped and took the
naughty animal home.

At 3:30 P.M. I went to Siegfriedstrasse and observed Wahnfried and its inhabitants from the entrance hall of a [nearby]
house. When I knew the place to be empty, I went to see the
beloved Master. He was sitting on the sofa in the salon, all
huddled over. I sat beside him. He kissed me and said, "I
have to think about you so much, and then I always worry
about you." I said, "Dear Master, as long as I am healthy I am
able to work steadily, and I am still young." He replied, "Oh,
that is not enough. Time and again I have to think of you,
and then I worry." He then asked, "What new pieces have
you recently studied in Pest?" I told him "Funérailles," which

68. For an account of Liszt's dental problems, see pp. 14–15.

I had learned mainly at his school [The Hungarian Royal Academy of Music, of which Liszt was the President]. He played on the table with his right hand and said (while pointing), "probably this exercise will loosen the fingers."

He coughed terribly and the blood rose to his head so strongly that his forehead became filled with bloodshot spots. I touched his brow and said, "Master, you have red spots here." He replied with such a childlike, tender look, "That is probably a rash!" The Master was infinitely sad and told me that he could not offer me anything happy here. "You don't even have a piano with which to divert yourself." I asked him to play cards with me. With much effort he got up from the sofa and sat down in the big armchair and said that Miska was to bring in the small table. Miska thought that we could play at the big table. The Master said to me, "I don't want to get angry [with Miska]; put the small table here. He has a thick head." We now played Écarté.[69] I had forgotten most of the game, and the Master explained it to me and won; but he was not as happy as when he usually won; he was infinitely sad and did not respond to my jokes. I told him that I had locked Belli up at home, and had beaten him again. "But you already punished the animal here," he said.

He soon fell asleep in the middle of the game with the cards in his hand. I sat down at the large table and wrote letters for a couple of hours, after which he woke up, and we continued to play. He fell asleep once more. I observed him like that for half an hour until he woke up; we had scarcely

69. Écarté is a card game for two players that uses a thirty-two-card deck.

played for five minutes when he fell asleep yet again. Now I quietly took away the small table (from in front of him), sat down at the large table, and read. After half an hour he awoke and said, "Why have you taken the small table away from me? I was just resting for a few minutes; let's continue to play." I put the small table back between us but saw that the game had become very, very difficult for him. I asked him to stop and to rest in bed, and he replied that he could do that. "You are staying with me?"

I told him about his cousin from the country who, because she had recently lost her lawsuit, wanted to ask the Master to remember her in his will. His relatives (the Wagners) already had enough money and, according to her, did not need his money as well. The Master said, *"I'll gladly give everything; regrettably I possess almost nothing, but if they like, I will give them my last coat."* These words he uttered with difficulty, broken off, and infinitely sadly. I had to pour water for him repeatedly (much to my annoyance). I told him that I did not like this at all. He had been too accustomed to wine since his youth in order to stop now; wine was the only thing left that would strengthen him. I thought that he was becoming weaker every day, and it was only the wretched water that was at fault. He reflected, "Well, you may be right, but wine has been forbidden me from all sides because of the dropsy, toward which I am supposed to be inclined. A doctor in Luxembourg whom I recently consulted completely shared your opinion. He said, 'Just continue to drink strong wines and cognac as well; your nature is too used to alcoholic beverages; you must not cease drinking wines if you want to conserve your health.'" The Master said, "The doctor made a very good impression on me, and I consider his opinion to be very reasonable. But what can I do against all of them!! By the way, you are complaining about your stomach. The Munkácsys, on doctor's orders, have sent me a superb cognac here. Have Miska bring it to your apartment. It will at least be of some use to you, and I am not allowed to drink it anyway."

I now asked him to lie down again, since talking was very difficult for him. We remained a while longer, each of us deeply saddened. We did not speak a single word and only held each other's hands tightly. It was getting dark, and the Master now asked to go to bed. Although the Master wanted to, he could not get up by himself from the chair and fell back again. I forcibly lifted him, his little body [*Körperchen*] was as heavy as lead, and I almost collapsed with him. Finally I had him standing up. He embraced me with a heavenly, thankful, and *deeply sad* gaze. Then he pressed a long kiss on my neck. I carried him closer to the bedroom (he could hardly place one foot in front of the other from weakness). There he immediately fell onto the chair in front of his bed. He called for Miska to undress him, but Miska was not to be found (the house was as if deserted). I offered to undress him, and he said, "That is exactly why they hate you and gossip so much about us; they begrudge me your help." I said, "But you are ill today, dear Master. Who could find anything wrong with my helping you now?" The Master said, "All of Bayreuth would be full of gossip tomorrow." I stood beside his little chair on which he sat and placed his poor, tired head against me. After a few moments he closed his eyes. I

ran to the flight of stairs to Fröhlich's and asked them to
have someone find Miska. I returned to the Master immediately and told him that someone was already looking for
Miska. The Master again laid his head against me and closed
his eyes. After waiting for quite some time, he began to undress himself. Finally Miska arrived and put him to bed.
When the Master was in bed, he called for me to come from
the salon and sit beside him. Miska brought the lamp, placed
it on the night table, and again went on his way. The Master
searched on the bedspread with his hand. I asked him what
he wanted, and he replied, "Give me your hand." I gave him
my left hand, which he then held tightly in his for the whole
evening. I now read to him from Wagner's writings. He
quickly fell asleep, but as soon as I had stopped reading he
gave a start and said, "I'm listening, just continue to read."
So I continued to read. Often in order to convince me that
he was really listening, he repeated my last word whenever I
made a pause. At 8:00 P.M. Miska brought dinner. It consisted of boiled chicken with rice. The Master did not want
to eat it, so I sat on his bed, held his plate for him, and said,
"Master, what would your mother say if she were to see that
her Franz was still the same? She would say, 'As with eating,
so with everything.'" He smiled sadly and now ate a little.[70]

70. Schmalhausen was well informed. Liszt had once written to his
mother: "Do you remember, dearest mother, a practical proverb that you
used to reproach me with when, as a youth, I showed little appetite: 'Lazy in
eating, lazy in everything.'" (LLBM, p. 118). Only Liszt himself could have
given Schmalhausen this reminiscence, and she here attempts to remind
the dying Liszt of it.

I put the meat on his fork and handed it to him. Soon he had had enough and left over half on the plate. Miska took the remainder out quickly. The Master said, "Run after him, perhaps you would like to eat it." I said that it would anger the fellow if I wanted it, and he would immediately eat it himself. The Master nodded, and said, "Then at least drink a little wine; just take my glass." After I had drunk, he himself took a hearty draught. I was quite monosyllabic, and the Master said repeatedly, "Why don't you say something." I felt, however, as if someone had bludgeoned me over the head, and I could think of nothing new to say. I told him, "Master, when you are in Pest again we will cook once more in our little kitchen." "Oh, yes," he said, "those lovely brains with onions again. If I could only get something like that here in the evening. It is easily digested at night. Munkácsy often has something like that." "Very good, Master, and when you are allowed to smoke again, we can have our cozy piquet games surrounded by a cloud of smoke." He suddenly looked up at me for a long time, completely changed, and said, "Tell me honestly, do you really believe that I'll be able to get up from here again?" (pointing to his bed). I said, "But Master, how can you talk like that; of course, everything will be all right within a few days." He coughed severely, brought up more phlegm into the handkerchief, and said, "I don't think so." He was boundlessly sad. I embraced him and said, "Then what will become of me!" He pressed me to himself and said, "Child, I have no confidence at all in the doctor and the many medicines. Every day I am told that things are getting better. I should have been healthy long ago; but I feel steadily weaker." I said, "I don't like the doctor either. He won't help you, but God will help you. I will pray for you." He looked at me sadly. "Isn't it true? You would not have believed that things were so bad with me. I suffered just as much in Luxembourg. I am pleased that you are here and can confirm it." "Indeed," I said, "this coughing, I would never have believed it." He raised his right hand high, extended the index finger, shook it back and forth, and said, "Yes, if I write something, it must be serious." He held my hand tightly in his; his whole body was boiling hot; he often nodded off to sleep but was very delirious. He spoke of wild dogs, roses, etc. He constantly hit the eiderdown with his hand, then abruptly woke up and said, "I know that I am saying a lot of confused things. I have a high fever. I always feel as if a wave were coming and I am in the water, and yet I know quite well that I am lying in bed. If only I were to be given an emetic, I think that would help me." Later the doctor came. I went into the adjoining room because the doctor wanted to examine the Master. As the doctor left he said there was no cause for alarm, only a severe cold. I sat down again beside the Master's bed, and he said, "Once again he thinks I am getting better."

The Master told me that Lassen had visited him early this morning on behalf of Fräulein von Schorn, who wanted to accompany him as his nurse to Kissingen. The Master said that he asked Lassen to inform her that the baroness [Meyendorff] was accompanying him there, and that should suffice. (He smiled while saying this.) Then he said, "I haven't attended church for a very long time; tomorrow read me something from the Book of Prayer. Admittedly, I know it by heart, but it calms me."

I told him that he would probably not sleep tonight. Had we been in Pest I would simply have sat up with him all night and kept him company. He replied, "It will be a bad night for me. I would be so pleased if you could stay, but that is impossible. Tomorrow all of Bayreuth would be aghast. Instead, leave me alone with my sad thoughts." I told him that if my staying with him would offend people, one of the younger individuals could sit up with him. The Master said, "From you I accept something like that, for I know that you do it gladly; but for them the night watch would be too strenuous." The Master sighed and said, "It was so lovely in Innsbruck with the Franciscan church and Defregger."[71] It was 11:00 P.M., and I said good night to him. He kissed me and said, "Come early tomorrow; my daughter will probably arrive around 6:30 A.M., so you can come around 7:30 A.M." I asked him if I should leave the lamp burning. He said, "Extinguish it, I am not used to it." I extinguished his lamp and went home with a heavy heart. How happily I would have stayed with him!

71. Liszt had spent several days at Innsbruck the previous October, where a seventy-fourth birthday concert had been given in his honor by the Innsbruck Male-Voice Choir, conducted by Franz Defregger. Lina had accompanied him to Innsbruck and had booked rooms for them both at the Hotel de l'Europe. There he had become emotional and had told her, "It is my last birthday, Linachen, I feel it; it is my last" (CBL-G).

Tuesday, July 27

I went to the Master after 7:00 A.M. and immediately Miska bellowed at me: Why hadn't I come earlier?; so far no one had been with the Master; he had been delirious the whole night and had been calling for me for a long time. I approached his bed, but I did not ask him how he was since I knew how much he disliked such questions. He looked at me completely exhausted and sadly reached for my hand, kissed it, and said, "Not better yet." He shook his head as he said it and looked at me with an indignant, I almost want to say childlike, look. I sat down by the bed. He told me that he had had an intense fever all night, and so far today no one had visited him. His daughter had not come either. Again he demanded, "Tell me something." Then he lifted his frail hand, counted with the fingers, and said, "Is it not correct, this month has thirty-one days?" I answered yes. "Well, good. Then you will leave here on the 2nd or rather the 1st [of August]. Since this month has thirty-one days, Frau von Meyendorff will arrive on the 2nd, and she must not see you here, otherwise she would raise difficulties not only with me (because I am ill) but also with my daughter. You will still receive some travel money from me." I said that

I did not need anything, that I had already received an abundance. He smiled and said, "An abundance!" The Master complained that he could not see or take leave of anyone. I replied that that was all very well, but none of them would ask him anything except "How are you?" and that would be dreadful for him. He said again, "If only I had fallen ill somewhere else. But to have to be ill right here, amid all this clamor, is really too stupid." He fell asleep again for a little while, and I read to him from Wagner's writings. Then Miska arrived and said that Cosima was outside, that I should go quickly into the salon so that she would not see me. But by no means did I want to avoid Cosima, and I even made a point of walking toward her. She brushed past me with a mute, hasty nodding of the head. I now waited in Miska's room; Stavenhagen also arrived. After an hour and a half Cosima emerged, greeted neither Stavenhagen nor me, and said to Miska, "Allow no one to see the abbé, and I mean *no one!*" Stavenhagen laughed mockingly and cut an angry face. As soon as she had left I went directly to the Master. Miska stole after me and said, "Right you are, the crazy witch has nothing to say." When I sat down beside his bed, the Master said, "I have just talked for half an hour with my daughter about you. It is the first time that I spoke with her about you. She of course knew the two lovely stories from Weimar already.[72] I thought that you were still in the room until just a few moments ago. I had not heard my daughter

72. Liszt's ironical reference to the "two lovely stories from Weimar" concerns the shoplifting charge brought against Lina and the thefts of money from Liszt's desk, mentioned in the prologue, pp. 6–9.

enter and so continued to speak to you about the baroness and about your departure, thinking that you were still here with me. Instead, you were not here at all, but rather my daughter."[73]

The Master now asked me whether my father had also been in Carlsbad and whether my brother was still ill and without a job. I noticed these questions because the Master had not asked me about my brother for eternities. The Master asked me whether I would go home for a few weeks from Bayreuth, since I had nothing to do during the summer in Pest, anyway. He said, "If you can stand it in Pest for another year I believe that you will succeed there." The Master fell asleep often and was delirious. He told us that Frau von Schorn had been to see his daughter today and had offered her services for the night watch. She had again assured his daughter of the tender feelings that bound her to the Master and that she would like to watch over him at night. The Master said, "My daughter answered that if night watches

73. We do not need to go beyond the little drama enshrined within these last three sentences to understand why Cosima felt both contempt and hostility toward Schmalhausen. Imagine the scene. Liszt is in bed, delirious, having uttered some intimate thoughts to Schmalhausen, who walks out just as Cosima walks in. Liszt continues talking to "Schmalhausen" and Cosima's ears start to burn. What she hears confirms much of the gossip surrounding Schmalhausen's relationship with her father: namely, that it is too close for comfort. And so she bans Schmalhausen from her father's presence. Cosima's knowledge of "the two lovely stories from Weimar" would not in itself have given Cosima pause; after all, she had known about them for some time. What appears to have shaken her, on the morning of July 27, was her father's obvious emotional attachment to the 22-year-old woman, which she had now witnessed at first hand.

were to become necessary the family itself would worry about them."[74]

The Master now told Miska that he wanted to get up for dinner; Miska was instructed to set places for the two of us on the small, round iron table in the bedroom. Then the Master got up, and I retired to the salon for the time being. He fetched me himself for the meal in the bedroom. We now sat down at the little iron table. Miska brought some steamed yellow carrots with a small slice of veal cutlet. The Master put almost all of it on my plate, since he could not eat. For me it was also impossible. This seemed to hurt his feelings, for he commented, "The meal is probably not so good." I devoured the carrots just to show him that it was in fact edible, only I looked toward the door in a feverish fear to make sure that no one was coming from Wahnfried, for then it would have been said that I was eating all the Master's food. The Master's hand shook badly; he coughed incessantly. We drank wine again from one glass (that is, water; everything was too strong for him). The Master said, "I should have taken to my bed the moment I arrived, then it would not have become so bad with me." He requested that he go to bed immediately after dinner, saying, "I am still too weak to stay up for long." After the Master had returned to bed he said, "Now

74. Cosima's refusal to accept Adelheid von Schorn's offer is confirmed by Schorn herself in her sensitive account of one of her last visits to Liszt's bedside. "I offered to undertake the necessary nursing duties," she wrote. "Frau Thode [Daniela] and Fräulein Eva Wagner accepted my offer with gratitude, but [Eva] later returned with word from Cosima; namely, that she 'wanted her father to be cared for exclusively by no one other than herself and her daughters'" (SZM, pp. 466–67).

read something for yourself; I will try to sleep for a little." It was not long before he asked, "What are you reading?" I replied: *"The Women of Weimar."* The Master said, "Written by Stahr, most likely?" I said no. "That's too bad," said the Master. "Tell Stahr when you see her that I am one of the few admirers of [Adolf] Stahr's work. The book is superb. Well now, go ahead and read something from yours." After a while the Master said impatiently, "The book is terribly boring. Observe the commas and new paragraphs more carefully!" I now stopped reading again and told him some news, that the Stahrs[75] were arriving today. The Master became somewhat cheered by this and said, "Yes, as soon as the baroness arrives we will immediately leave for Pest. There we will pick up the cousin from the country, and the three of us will go to Kissingen." When I looked at him with surprise, he

---

75. Dr. Adolf Stahr (1805–76), the prominent German historian, had been a professor at the University of Jena. His book *Jena und Weimar* had turned him into a national authority on these two cities. Stahr's two spinster daughters, Anna (1835–1909) and Helene (1838–1914), had been among Liszt's closest acquaintances during the Weimar years. They lived in a small cottage on Schwanenseestrasse and were celebrated for their Sunday afternoon "at homes," which Liszt often attended in the company of friends and pupils. Liszt used to joke that no matter how many people he brought with him, the elastic rooms of the small cottage would expand to meet any emergency (LL, p. 78). As they bustled around the cottage, serving cakes and coffee, they created the illusion that they were in all the rooms simultaneously —a cause of some hilarity among their guests. Anna and Helene Stahr were regarded as eccentric by the local population and were dubbed "the Starlings." Carl Lachmund tells us that the two sisters dressed exactly alike, "carefully and neatly attired in the style of schoolgirls at a Sunday-school picnic" (LL, p. 75). Despite all the outward appearances of fluttering superficiality, the Stahr sisters were, in fact, highly cultivated and had inherited their father's love of learning and attachment to the arts.

laughed heartily and said, "Well, that would suit the baroness just fine."[76]

I continued to read to him from the "boring" book, and he fell soundly asleep. Before that, he asked me, "What did your mother write to you yesterday?" I told him the approximate contents, among other things that I was reputedly reveling in one pleasure after another here. He said, "What reveling I am offering you! Were I not ill, it would be different for you; but like this it is miserable!" I sat beside his bed for half an hour, and he slept. Suddenly Daniela came in. She did not dare to speak because the Master was sleeping. I stood up, showed her the place where I had stopped reading, and she took over my place at his bedside. I left quietly. Outside Miska was snoring. For a long time I remained standing behind the door. The Master soon awoke. Daniela wanted to continue reading. He asked, "That is not Lina, who is there?" Daniela answered and continued to read. He said that she read incomprehensibly; he seemed dissatisfied. Daniela stayed by the bed for another ten minutes. When she began to leave, I crept away so that she would not see me

---

There are two near-illegible lines at this point in the diary in which Liszt refers to a book called *Wippschen* which he says is being read a lot in Bavaria. The name "Wippschen" refers to jokes or pranks.

76. Considering Liszt's desperate physical condition, this was a surprising flash of humor. Those who knew Baroness Meyendorff described her as cold and aloof, the last person who might be expected to get on with someone as rustic as Liszt's "cousin from the country." In any case, the plans for Kissingen were already in place—as Liszt well knew. He and Schmalhausen were smiling at the prospect of seeing Olga von Meyendorff's demeanor upon being told that all these plans had been set aside and that this joyful trio would now take off for the spa together.

still standing there. It was 3:00 P.M. When I returned at 4:00 P.M. Miska said that Cosima had forbidden entrance to everyone, that today I could not see him. I had the feeling that I would never be allowed to see him again. I went home in a despairing mood and wrote to a few of our friends about the Master.

Wednesday, July 28

Very early, around 6:00 A.M., I was called out of bed by the Fröhlich's servant girl. She said that I was to come to Miska at once. I assumed that the Master was asking for me, and I flew to Siegfriedstrasse. When I arrived there, breathless, Miska said, "Kissasonge [a term of endearment for Lina],[77] why did you hurry so? There's no rush; I was only to tell you something from the Master. He greets you very warmly and tells you that he has been forbidden to see anyone; you, too, are not allowed to go to him, and he thought that you might as well leave the city. You would just be bored here, and in any case the baroness is arriving soon and then you would have to leave anyway. The Master wants to tell you that he will write to you as soon as he has recovered. You will be the first to receive a letter (he said that in a drawn-out way). I am also instructed to give you travel money." I was deeply hurt to be offered travel money through his servant, especially

77. Lina simply copied down this unusual word as she heard it, perhaps not realizing that it was the corrupt Hungarian noun "Kisasszonyka," which is the equivalent in German of Fräuleinchen, or "little young lady." To judge from her relations with Miska in general, she would hardly have welcomed such a patronizing epithet.

since I had *never* asked Liszt for a penny. I told Miska that I did not need any money, that he should greet the Master warmly from me and tell him that I would not depart Bayreuth until he had completely recovered. I now remained in Miska's room, resolved not to leave the house. Even if I could not remain in the Master's room, I at least wanted to hear from outside what was happening to him. He had had a very bad night and had slept throughout the whole day with only a few interruptions. During the day Cosima came to him a few times for a few minutes to read to him with her cold, measured voice about Wagner. Doctor Fleischer[78] came at 3:30 P.M. from Erlangen and said that the Master had been suffering from pneumonia for the past week and should remain completely quiet, and not be allowed to speak much. With this advice the wise doctor departed. As a result, no one was allowed into the Master's room during the afternoon either, in spite of his many calls, and the Glorious One [*der Herrliche*] remained alone with his morbid thoughts for the whole afternoon and night (even Miska did not watch over him, and a sister of mercy [*eine barmherzige Schwester*] was not accepted either). The evening before, Stavenhagen had attached himself to Eva in Wahnfried, where there was a big soirée and the young girls were "receiving," and through her he had gained entrance to the Master's bedroom—in spite of the fact that the Master did not want to see him at all. Eva and Isolde were supposed to

78. Dr. Fleischer was professor of medicine at nearby Erlangen University. His purpose from this point in the drama was to deliver a second opinion to that of the attending physician Dr. Landgraf.

take turns, standing in the salon in order to hear when the Master needed anything; this, however, was *very boring* for the two girls; they armed themselves with novels and allowed Stavenhagen to flirt with them. The Master repeatedly called for Eva; he wanted to know how the previous evening had turned out in Wahnfried. Eva said, "Mr. Stavenhagen performed your 'Franziskus' [presumably one of the Franciscan Legends] wonderfully yesterday, but please Grandfather, don't ask any more, since it is harmful for you." "You are a completely bad crowd," said the Master, in that divine tone of his, "that you leave me so alone here." Eva returned to the salon with Stavenhagen and invited him to dine with her. At 3:00 P.M. Stavenhagen had come smugly along the street, where I stood trembling beside a fence and said to me, "I haven't dined this well for a long time: five courses; Eva is a fabulous girl." I asked him, "How is the Master? You were fortunate enough to see him." He said, "I'm not with the old man at all; rather with Eva in the salon; besides, the old man sleeps continually." And with that he went on his way, whistling.

Thursday, July 29

That night I could not sleep because of the anguish I felt for the beloved Master. About 7:00 A.M. I sent for Miska. He said that Cosima would watch beside the Master during the nights from now on (i.e. she had ordered a bed to be set up in the salon, much to the chagrin of himself and the Fröhlichs). She was making a mess of the whole salon with her featherbeds and the laundry; and besides, it was only an "act," for the benefit of others, that she was moving in here, since she was in any case not watching over the Master at his bedside. She used to arrive in the evenings about 11:00 P.M., would immediately undress and go to bed; and because she had tightly shut the door leading to the Master's bedroom, she was unable to hear if the Master requested anything. Early at 6:00 A.M. she would again run to the theater and would remain there the whole day. Isolde and Eva would come at 11:00 A.M. and they would not enter the bedroom either but would amuse themselves with Stavenhagen in the salon.) "Yes, yes," said Miska, "Kissasonge, I am watching that nothing happens to the Master, for they would be happy (he pointed to Wahnfried) if he expired here and never left Bayreuth." Frau Fröhlich joined in and said, "Yes, I believe that as well; they would be content; they are heartless toward the old gentleman. I can't sleep at night. My bedroom is above that of the old gentleman, and his moaning and rattling cuts me to the quick, and I don't even know him. Last night he groaned terribly. I wept uncontrollably." The woman said, "You know, one would be inclined to believe that he was your grandfather and not theirs over there; you seem to love the old gentleman a great deal." Of course, the woman had no idea what I was actually thinking and feeling—I who had sat by his bed day and night, most recently in Rome and Pest, who had served him each drink and to whom the Master had become so accustomed that he could not fall asleep unless I sat beside his bed, prayed with him, and he had put his hands in mine. And now I had to loiter outside, knowing him to be alone, without help; he, who had a heart in such need of love, and so longed for someone to take care of him! I went into Miska's room again in order at least to hear the Master's voice through the door.

Eva arrived around 10:00 A.M. (the young girls did not arrive earlier, even though the Master did not sleep at all during the entire night and the long morning!). Stavenhagen accompanied Eva. The Master said to her and Stavenhagen, "Help me get up a bit; I am so bed-sore." With a sharp, snappy, and heartless voice this monster of a grandchild said, "Grandpapa, I beg you, don't be so *childish* to want to get up in your condition. I don't understand you." The Master: "But at least until my bed is made. You can't believe how sore I am." Eva in a mocking voice: "Just wait until Mama arrives. She will tell you what you have to do." The Master wept and said, half imploring, half commanding, "But I want to get out of bed." He made attempts with his feet to crawl out of bed. Stavenhagen forced him back. So he now said to Stavenhagen, "Call Miska for me." What I suffered behind the door! I wanted to rush in, knock these inhuman people down, to calm him, caress him, and to fulfill his proper wishes. What a punishment I felt it to be, that no bond of kinship tied me to him that would entitle me to care for him!

Miska arrived, and the Master told Eva, "One moment, Eva." She thought that her grandfather wanted [   ][79] and went out. He leaned up in bed for a moment. Miska handed him the [container], but he said quietly, "not necessary, I just wanted to ask about Lina. Have you spoken to her? What does she say, and what will she do? Did you give her my message? I would like to speak with her for a few moments, absolutely, yes absolutely." Embarrassed, Miska said, "Everything is taken care of, Your Grace." The Master wanted to continue speaking, but Miska ran immediately to the salon door and called Eva. When Miska came out, I asked him, "The Master mentioned my name, what were you supposed to tell me?" Miska said, "Just let me go, Kissasonge, you are mistaken. The Master said nothing about you." (The blackguard did not believe that not a single word of the Master escaped me.) Miska returned again to the Master. Stavenhagen and Eva were standing at the foot of the bed. The Master now invented a different ruse to enable him to get up. He said to Miska, "I haven't been shaved for such a long

79. Schmalhausen's hiatus. The context suggests that the missing words were "wanted to use the chamber pot."

time; shave me." Miska finally came with warm water, etc. The Master said, "Well, it will be difficult for you to shave me in bed; that won't work; I would prefer to get up for it." Miska said no, it is better in bed.

Lessmann and Mihalovich came in and both stood with me at the door. When they heard that the Master was being shaved, they laughed mockingly and said, "How can one still wish to be shaved?" And Lessmann with the greatest calm: "He won't ever get up again," and with that they both went on their way. The Master remained patiently in bed while being shaved, then he said decisively, "There, now I really *want* to get up; Miska, you will help me." Miska thought, "Perhaps the Master would recover after all," and he did not dare to push the Master's anger to the extreme. So he replied, "Right away, Your Grace," then took the shoes from in front of the Master's bed and said, "I'll be right back. I'm just going to polish the shoes." He went out and of course did not return. Eva enjoyed this dishonest trick, and she returned calmly to the salon. The Master was too weak to get up by himself, and the heartless creature knew it.

I looked through the crack in the door. The Master was lying on his pillows crying, completely emaciated. At this moment I felt that he was "King Lear."[80] I now left for a few hours and thought to myself, "At 4:00 P.M. I will return; then they will all be in the theater again. I will be on the lookout,

80. Liszt's disciple Alexander Gottschalg reported that Liszt broke a windowpane by throwing a glass of seltzer water through it in the hope that the cold night air would hasten his end. This information reached him from one of the Stahr sisters who had seen Liszt on Friday, July 30 (GFLW, p. 157).

just as I was on Monday at the Master's request, and when they have all left I will go to him; then he won't lie so alone in his fever and his fear." I carried out this thought. After everyone had driven off to the theater I went to the Master's house, rang six times, but no one showed themselves. I now crept into the garden and climbed up to the window of the salon. I saw Stavenhagen sitting in the salon, and the door to the Master's bedroom was *closed*. I implored him to let me gain access to the Master for a few minutes, but he said no and asked, "Was it you who had rang so much just now? Cosima has locked us all in and has taken the key with her to the theater, so that we *can't* let anyone in here. Thus, I am also locked in and furious about it, since I wanted to go to the theater. If she does not return soon I will leave through the window. Until now I have been writing letters." I asked how the Master was. He said again, "The old man is sleeping; besides, in a few days he will have recovered completely, and we will be playing whist with him again." I cried like a child and begged Stavenhagen to help me to get through the window into the salon. (It was only a small jump.) Stavenhagen said, "Cosima is bound to return at any moment and what would she say, if she were to find me locked in with you?" I considered this and thought to myself, "The insinuation of this stupid boy! I don't care what Cosima thinks. But this could mean trouble for the Master, even on his sickbed, and this I do not want." I climbed back and ran like a dog who has lost his master up and down the street in front of the house. Then the Fröhlichs' servant girl met me. "Don't let them laugh at you," she said. "Yesterday Miska and Staven-

hagen were already looking forward to your arriving and
finding all the doors locked. They locked themselves in and
even requested my mistress to tell you that she saw Cosima
take the keys with her."

Everyone was at the theater. I sat down on the stone steps
in the Master's little garden for five hours and brooded. I
went up the few steps and thus reached the small arbor directly in front of the Master's bedroom, so that only the thin
glass door was separating us; otherwise, I would have been
at his bedside. The bed was only separated from the large
glass door by the night table. I was therefore able to observe
him carefully.

How I wish I could have knocked on the windowpane, have
him recognize me. He would then have jumped out of bed
immediately and unlocked the door for me, but then I would
also have had to give up this coign of vantage. Joukowsky[81]
came to relieve Stavenhagen, who then went to the theater

81. Paul von Joukowsky (1845–1912) had designed the stage sets for the
first performance of *Parsifal*, in 1882, and had become a prominent member of the Bayreuth circle. Attracted by his "modernistic" approach to portrait painting, Liszt had commissioned Joukowsky to execute a portrait of
himself, which the composer then dispatched to the Toronto-based piano
manufacturers Mason and Risch, in return for Vincent Risch having sent
him one of the company's first grand pianos. Joukowsky's portrait created
such a sensation that the grand duke of Weimar commissioned a smaller
copy, which eventually found its way to Canada as well. For a fuller account
of this story, and the fate of the portraits, see WFL, vol. 3, pp. 423–24. The
larger of the two portraits is reproduced in BFL, p. 286, where it is wrongly
attributed to the Toronto Conservatory of Music. See also KLMR, esp. pp.
79–82 and 89–90.

During the festival, Joukowsky actually rented rooms in the same house
as Liszt himself (no. 1 Siegfriedstrasse), which were situated immediately

No. 1 Siegfriedstrasse, the house where Liszt died.

(it was 6:00 P.M.). Joukowsky opened the door of the salon to the Master's bedroom, left it ajar, and sat down in the salon. From the arbor, as soon as the door to the Master's room was opened, I could also survey the salon. The Master now raised himself up in bed and said several times, "Is no one there, then?" No answer. He now remained propped up in bed and

above those of the Master. He was a daily witness to Liszt's slow decline toward death.

Detail of No. 1 Siegfriedstrasse.

looked toward the door to the salon for a long time. Then he fell back in his pillows with a sigh, disheartened. How painfully all this cut into my soul. I threw myself on the stone steps and cried bitterly and begged God to let me see and speak to him at least just once more. I remained in the garden from 4:00 to 9:00 p.m. and heard the Master's constant moaning. Suddenly the Fröhlichs' servant girl crept up to me and said, "Fräulein, risk it. Joukowsky has just left, Miska is sleeping, Stavenhagen is writing letters, the doors are open, and they believe that you are long gone." Like a nervous feline I crept stealthily to the Master's bedside. Miska was just entering the bedroom and threatened me with his fist, saying, "Just wait, you'll be in for it later." I ignored the blackguard and stood in front of the Master's bed. He felt the fresh stream of air; his eyes were almost completely shut; he could not see me any more. The Master had become thin during the last few days. He said, weak and vexed, *"Que voulez-vous?"* (he thought that I was one of the grandchildren). I replied, "It's me, Lina." He awoke as if from a dream, spread his arms around me, and said, "Oh, Lina." He was moved with joy and said, "Come, sit by me, you poor child. I am not allowed to see you, and you suffer?" My hands were trembling like leaves, my whole body was shaking, and my teeth were chattering. I felt that this was the last time God would allow me to hold him in my arms. Yes, at this moment it became a certainty for me, an inner voice said to me to make use of this moment, and I kissed him like one can only kiss the most precious thing on earth for the last time. I could not weep; I knew that he must not be excited. The pain so choked my throat that I was incapable of stammering a word. He said again, "Sit down" (motioning with his hand). "You are trembling." Stavenhagen stood behind the one door and Miska by the other. I told the Master that I only wanted to embrace him once and had to leave right away, that I must not be seen with him. I was in the highest fever; the most heavenly joy and pain had so merged within me at this moment that I was not in command of my words at all, and as if infatuated with him constantly said "Du" to him [i.e., the informal address]. The two good friends heard this and certainly thought that I always addressed the Master in this intimate way. How I came to do all this I still cannot explain, even today. I was simply completely entranced and in an exhalted state. The Master asked, "Have you been given the 100 gulden? It has been tormenting me for so long whether you have received it, otherwise you won't have enough to make do. They have rummaged around my wallet so much already."

I replied that so far I had not received anything. He called out vehemently, "Miska, you assured me that you gave Fräulein Schmalhausen the money." Miska made a sign toward me and said, "It has been taken care of already, Your Grace." The Master said, "It has not been taken care of, give it to me immediately. And is N.T. written on the envelope? That stands for Táborszky."[82] Then turning to me, "I am still in his debt, dear Lina, and you will be so good as to return

82. Nándor Táborszky (1831–88) was one of Liszt's Hungarian publishers. From the context, it appears that Liszt was creating a deception, placing Táborszky's name on an envelope containing money that was really meant for Lina.

the money to him when you go back to Pest." (While saying this the Master pressed my hand meaningfully; in spite of his fever he knew very well that Miska and Stavenhagen ought not to see that he was giving me money.) While Miska went to fetch the money, and Stavenhagen remained at the door, the Master motioned to me to bend over him and said, "Find out whether Göllerich has received anything. He is so needy, and I have sent him something. The Master said again to sit down (pointing to the chair by his bed): "You must forgive them for not allowing you to see me, otherwise everyone would want to come. She just left" (meaning his daughter) "so you can easily stay with me for a couple of hours before anyone comes back." Stavenhagen now indicated that I should leave, that the Master had slept soundly until now. Frau Wagner would surely arrive at any moment, he said, and then they would be lost for having allowed me to see the Master. The Master said, "Lina, stay here, and hold my hand; my daughter really won't return for another two hours." Stavenhagen said softly, "He has been sleeping until now; come along, he does not know what he is saying." Miska then called out, "That's enough, now!" The Master raised himself up and said with a threatening voice, "Is someone here, then?" Miska said timidly, "No one, Your Grace." The Master said, "That I know as well." Then he ordered, "Go out, and close the door." Miska went out with a hangdog look, while Stavenhagen eavesdropped at the salon door. The Master became delirious again. He sat upright in bed and suddenly said, "Good Lina, you are half Bavarian. Do you know when the birthday of the unlucky king is? No one wants to tell me!"

Regrettably I did not know it and said so. "Too bad," he said sadly. "I was hoping that you would tell me."[83] His room was completely dark, a dim night lamp burned at the end of the room and was the only illumination. Stavenhagen now called quietly and fearfully, "Cosima is coming." I pressed the Master to me, as if I wanted to wrest him from death. He said, "Don't leave me, she won't be back for a long time. I ran out, believing that Cosima was on the way. Stavenhagen said that she was not there yet, but would arrive at any moment. "Leave the old man now, he just talks a lot of nonsense, like that about the king of Bavaria just now." (I knew the Master to be mentally more fit than the whole heartless lot of them.) Again, I heard the Master's weak voice call out, "Lina!" Miska tried to hold on to me, but I tore myself away abruptly and once again rushed to the Master. He asked hurriedly, "When are you leaving?" "Not until you are fully recovered," I said. "Just don't let her [Meyendorff] see you," he said, "for she is arriving any day."[84] "Master, as soon as the baroness arrives I will not leave my house, for your sake; she will not even meet me on the street. And even if you should have to lie in bed for weeks, I will not leave Bayreuth until

83. The "unlucky king" was Ludwig II of Bavaria, and his approaching birthday fell on August 25. Ludwig's death by suicide, which had occurred on June 13, has already been remarked, and it had clearly affected Liszt. See pp. 53–54. About the topic of Liszt's superstitions and premonitions, an entire chapter could be written.

84. Liszt was referring to Baroness Meyendorff who, like Cosima, could not abide to be in the same room with Lina Schmalhausen. Like Cosima, too, she preferred to think that she knew better than Liszt himself what company he ought to keep.

you have fully recovered." He took my hand and smiled and said, "That's how I like it. Weeks? Oh no, I've been taking good care of myself for three weeks already; in two or three days at most I will be completely healthy again." "Well then," I said trembling, "I'll see you before the baroness does. And I won't have to say good-bye." "Stay a little longer," the Master said. But I pressed him to me once more and rushed out. Outside I ran up and down the street like a wounded animal. I had plenty of time to regret my credulity and my stupidity. The Master was right. Cosima only returned three hours later, around 11:30 P.M. How much happier I would have been spending these hours with him, instead of standing alone in front of his house in the dark night.

Around midnight, when everything at the Master's was quiet, I went into the Traube[85] where all the students had gathered—Thomán, Stavenhagen, the Stahrs, etc.—cracking their usual jokes until two o'clock in the morning. Stavenhagen raised a glass of beer toward me and said, "Well, you can thank me for allowing you to stay with the Master for so long. Miska wanted to carry you out of the door, but I prevented him from doing that." (So it had come to this, that the youngest student of the Master—Stavenhagen had only been with Liszt for nine months—was giving me permission whether or not I could see him!!!) "By the way," Stavenhagen continued, "The old man was still calling for you, and when you did not come he asked me whether you had actually left already."

85. A local tavern.

Friday, July 30

Early, I walked back and forth in front of the Master's house. I was not allowed inside anymore. Miska permitted no one to enter. I only learned what was going on through the Fröhlichs' servant girl. She told me that the Master had had a terrible night. He no longer ate anything and would accept only soda water to drink. The Master was unconscious a great deal. Today Göllerich was allowed to alternate with Stavenhagen in the salon—the lucky people! (Göllerich had been sick in bed until the day before yesterday.) At 4:00 P.M. everyone was again at the theater. In the Traube at noon I had asked Göllerich to let me into the salon during the afternoon for a few minutes. I did not want to speak to the Master, only to hear his voice behind the door. I tried my luck and went to the house. The doors were all locked. I went into the garden again and quietly called below the window: "Göllerich!" I received no answer. Stavenhagen came to the window and said, "I can't let you in." I had thought more highly of Göllerich than of Stavenhagen. Göllerich had promised to let me in at noon. He had me to thank for his whole position with the Master, and I now counted on his gratitude. I jumped up to the window. Göllerich was sitting on a chair and ran away. I now went back to the outside door. There I rang so violently that the Master had to hear it (nothing made any difference to me now). Those strange fellows were allowed to see the Glorious One, to be around him, while I, who had sat by his bed day and night, was forced to remain on the street like a dog.

Stavenhagen now came out, opened the door, and said, "What's the idea? The Master will wake up from your ringing." "What you are allowed to do I have been doing for a long time," was my reply, and I stepped into the salon. Miska now quickly locked the door to the Master's room adjoining the salon and his own. I remained seated in the salon. Stavenhagen now wanted to go to the theater, but his hat was in Miska's room. He knocked at the latter's door and said, "Miska, open up." But the fellow said, "Not until she has left" (meaning me). After Stavenhagen became coarse at the door and said, "Damn it, give me my hat." Miska threw Stavenhagen's hat through a crack in the door; he then went off to the theater singing. Göllerich, who for certain reasons had to remain Miska's friend, as did all of the young people who became popular with the Master through the servant, sat there completely cowed, not knowing whose side to take.

I saw that my waiting was completely unsuccessful and left in despair. I went for a walk to the Jean Paul Haus,[86] where I had sat so often with d'Albert (four years ago!). There I had a good cry. Around 7:00 P.M. I went to the Master's house

86. Jean Paul Richter (1763–1825), the German Romantic poet, had lived in Bayreuth for the last twenty years of his life. He is buried in Bayreuth's Stadtfriedhof, not far from Liszt.

again. Göllerich was now patroling there, as well as the Stahrs and Merian.[87] Cosima with daughters and son were all at the theater. Göllerich felt unwell and left too. When I asked him who was with the Master he answered, "No one."

The Stahrs then went in to Miska and remained for ten minutes. Miska led them to the Master's bedside. Both came out weeping and said, "He does not recognize us anymore and rattles terribly. He will die tonight. If only it would be over quickly for him. He suffers so dreadfully. No one is with him who lovingly holds his hand and calms him." This time the old gossip sisters were right. I forced my way into the Master's room (Miska thought that I was off and away. When he saw me he became frightened). I said to him, "You are a great blackguard. We are going to have a reckoning later." He wanted to kiss my hand and stuttered, "You don't know how sorry I am for you, but I will lose my job if I allow you to enter." I did not answer him and stood at the foot of the Master's bed. The Master's eyes were shut tight; he sat upright in bed and moaned horribly. I did not dare to address him, perhaps he could have died, for he was breathing his last, and then Miska and the others would have said that I frightened him and therefore murdered him. The Master was emaciated like a straw. Since his eyes were tightly closed he did not see me. His whole body shook, as if in the grip of a strong frost. Between his teeth he murmured, "Miska, what

87. Emilie ["Mici"] Genast-Merian (1833–1905) was a gifted singer and a daughter of the former Weimar stage manager, Eduard Genast. Liszt had known her well during the Weimar years. It was for her that he had composed some of his songs.

time?" "Nine o'clock, Your Grace." "Today I feel very ill. Is today Thursday?" The *donkey* said, "No, Friday." Liszt sank back into the pillows and echoed, "Friday."[88]

I did not budge from my place. To startle him might have meant his death. Miska entreated me to leave again because someone could come at any moment. I left, but with what a heart! In the outer corner of the window a night lamp burned. Otherwise everything was pitch black. I then went out without having spoken to the Master. Outside, Merian and the Stahrs were waiting for me. For the first time in her life Merian was cordial toward me and said, "May he be granted peace; he has had such great pleasures in London and France during the evening of his life. Grant him peace." I snapped at her indignantly and said, "If you call that peace, when your body is decaying and putrefying in the graveyard. I don't wish such peace on my greatest enemy, much less on him." She said, "You are still too young to understand me. I wish from the bottom of my heart that you may bear this blow, and that God will give you the strength to continue living." But she had to weep. She told the Stahrs that Liszt had always helped her child so benevolently, which obligated her to thank him.

88. It was well known among Liszt's friends and pupils that he was superstitious. Earlier, on New Year's Eve, while he was still in Rome, he had been in the middle of a game of whist when the clock stopped ticking. Liszt immediately observed: "One of us will die this year." He then went on to point out that New Year's Day itself fell on a Friday, and that his next birthday (October 22) would likewise fall on a Friday. This confluence of days and dates he declared to be a bad omen and concluded that the year 1886 would be an unlucky one for him (GL, p. 122).

The Wagners today were attending a performance of *Parsifal*. There they were moved by a puppet theater, while the living Amfortas was here, struggling with death on his sickbed.

The previous day I had chosen for myself a place for the night vigil in the garden. The Master's bedroom faced the garden; he was situated on the ground floor. A large glass door led to some stone steps that led to the garden. There on the steps I prepared my night accommodation. Miska must have suspected something, and in his vileness had lowered the blinds. Luckily they did not reach all the way down, and I was left with a small slit through which I could survey the whole room.

I got some felt shoes, packed myself into a thick coat, pulled a scarf over my head, slipped some cognac into my pocket, and went to my hiding place! It was 9:30 P.M. Miska was sleeping. Not far from the bed the Fröhlichs' servant girl was sitting. It was very dark in the room. The Master was delirious, and when he awoke he probably saw a woman's skirt. He said, "Lina, come closer, don't be afraid, it's only me," and at the same time in his fever he threw his hands on the bedspread and beat time. Then he fell asleep again. Suddenly he pushed his feet out of bed and said, "Lina, I have to go now, I have to go, child, come along." The Master then wanted to get out of bed. He spread his arms out and wished to approach the figure, since it did not come to him. The girl now became truly frightened, ran to Miska, and woke him up. Miska came to the Master and put him back into bed. The girl came out to see me; she knew of my hiding place, and said, "Fräulein, the old gentleman has already started his journey; he will die tonight."

The Master now became increasingly delirious and hallucinated about Wagner's music in Antwerp. He told himself long stories in French. Thus it got to be 11:30 P.M. The doctor came and waited for Frau Wagner in the adjoining room. She arrived around midnight and went directly into the salon. There she spoke with the doctor for ten minutes. Then she closed her door leading to the Master's room (without once having gone to the bedside of her father, without pressing a kiss on his forehead and feeling his pulse!) and immediately went to bed, extinguishing the lamp. For the first time it was decided that it would probably be better if Miska would watch during the night beside the Master's bed. The fellow had placed an upholstered easy chair in the Master's room, threw himself on it, and of course immediately began to snore like a saw [*Säge*]. The Master was often startled; then in his fever he spoke a lot of muddled things. Around 1:00 A.M. he quietly called, "Miska, are you awake?" Miska continued to snore and the Master repeated, "Miska, Miska" at least eight times. *Finally*, after twenty minutes, Miska woke up. The Master wanted the chamber pot. Miska lifted him from the bed. Outside the moon shone brightly, and it illuminated the room. I saw the Master's bare feet, thin and shivering as he fell back onto the bed (he was too weak to stand). After he was in bed again he said quietly, "I thank you; please continue sleeping."

At 2:00 A.M. the Master leaped out of bed like a madman, clutching his heart, and shouting so horribly that it could be heard across the neighborhood. He could not breathe and thought he was choking to death. These cries of terror went on for half an hour. Miska wanted to get the Master to bed again, but he had incredible strength. Cosima got dressed and sent for the doctor, who arrived after one-and-a-half hours. When he arrived at the bedside, the Master was lying diagonally across the bed, motionless, where he had collapsed from the pain. The doctor said that he was dead (the Master was ice cold). Only after massaging him for a long time did the limbs warm up, and he was given Hoffmann's drops. The doctor then left again. From now on Liszt remained unconscious.

Saturday, July 31

The next morning Dr. Fleischer was cabled (*finally*, but too late!). Until now, during the entire week of his illness [Liszt] had only been given mineral water to drink. (I have always heard that one should pamper such patients with cognac and champagne!) Cosima, for the first and only time, remained at the Master's bedside for the whole day. The Master ate nothing anymore. Around 4:00 P.M. in the afternoon, the doctor from Erlangen arrived.[89] The whole family was present in the salon. The doctor said that the coming night would be crucial, that the crisis was approaching, and that if Liszt made it through the night he would be saved. Now, as a foremost consideration, the heaviest wines and champagnes were prescribed and poured into the Master. He, the divine person, permitted *everything* to be done for him, like a willing child. He came to for a few seconds and gave Dr. Fleischer his hand (but did not speak). He *wanted* to speak, but his lips were tightly baked together. Cosima tried to catch the words; she bent down over him, but he could no longer make himself understood. (On Friday

89. This was the aforementioned Dr. Fleischer, who was on the medical faculty of Erlangen University.

night, when a kitchen servant who was a stranger was sitting by his bed, Frau Wagner could have heard much from him!) Daniela, Isolde, Eva, and Siegfried now left. Siegfried went over to Wahfried and sat on an upstairs windowsill and read. (This child had the heart to sit quietly upon a windowsill pursuing his novel while his grandfather was in the throes of death.) Around 8:30 P.M. a cozy dinner was offered at Wahnfried. Stavenhagen was invited to join them.

I bundled myself up, as on the previous night, and stood at the Master's balcony door. Cosima and Dr. Fleischer sat by the Master's bedside. The doctor constantly felt the Master's pulse, while in his other hand he held a pocket watch. At the other end of the room sat the bungler from Bayreuth, Dr. Landgraf. The Master moaned until 10:30 P.M., then he was completely calm, but his breathing was heavy. Around 11:00 P.M. I saw both doctors bending over his bed, holding two large silver candelabras, which they then put back on the night table. I was perplexed. The whole room was illuminated, although regrettably I could not see the Master's head—only the chest, arms, and the whole lower part of the body. At 11:15 P.M. the Master received two morphine injections in the region of the heart. The odor penetrated all the way to my window.[90] Then the Master's body *shook* violently

90. Unless Schmalhausen was later to confirm from independent sources the nature of the substance injected into Liszt, we doubt that it could have been morphine, which has no perceptible smell. To be sure, morphine would have been the drug of choice as a painkiller. But some sources claim that Liszt's doctors administered injections of camphor to warm the body. Camphor has a highly characteristic aroma which could easily have drifted toward Lina's coign of vantage.

as if an earthquake were taking place. The bedcover flew rapidly up and down, then his left arm fell along the bed. The doctors again bent over him with the candelabras, set them down again, and left the room *without saying a single word*. Cosima knelt down in front of the bed (from this position I could observe her face). She was completely calm; not the slightest trace of emotion was visible on her marble face. For a *long,* long time she looked at the Master's left hand (yes, she stared at the hand with curiosity). Then she put it under the bedspread and caressed his upper arm tenderly. She continued to kneel in front of the bed for another ten minutes, folded her hands, and prayed. Isolde entered, knelt down in front of the bed, embraced her mother, and went out again. For a few moments Cosima laid her body diagonally across the Master's feet on the bed; then she sat down on a chair at the foot of the bed, folded her hands, and fell asleep in that position. Her head fell first to the right, then to the left, then to the front. Then she would wake up with a start, breathe deeply, and continue to sleep. I was quite content. I thought that the Master had received his injection and was now in a deep sleep, that tomorrow he would wake up with renewed strength and he would have survived the night.[91] To think of death would have been ridiculous,

91. It is clear from this part of her narrative that Schmalhausen had no idea that Liszt had just died. This blow would not fall upon her until the following morning. And this raises a small, but intriguing technical matter. Schmalhausen states that Liszt's doctors gave him two injections in the region of the heart at 11:15 P.M. In light of the dramatic response of his body (to whatever was injected into it), Liszt was still alive at that time—and presumably did not expire for several more minutes. But the death register in

for Cosima was sleeping beside his bed and nothing was stir-
ring in the room. Had he died one surely would have heard
the sound of voices. But the scene was so peaceful. Cosima
was not weeping; on the contrary: she sat there as if she were
guarding his sleep. I remained at the window until 4:30 A.M.,
and as I was watching Cosima I thought, "You are not happy."
Cosima never stopped sighing heavily; she seemed fatigued
and weary of living. I feared that she might recognize me
from my shadow, for day was about to break, and she often
looked anxiously toward the window where I stood. So I
crept away quietly.

---

the Bayreuth archives states that the time of death also occurred at 11:15
P.M. Were the doctors themselves the immediate cause of Liszt's death? An
injection of either morphine or camphor introduced into the heart muscle
by mistake would have resulted in Liszt's swift demise. Lina had earlier described Dr. Landgraf as "a bungler"—a description we see no cause to mod-
ify as a result of everything we learn about him from this sorry sequence of
events. He had, after all, pronounced Liszt dead a full twenty hours before
his patient had actually expired.

Through a misreading of Lina Schmalhausen's handwriting I had always
concluded that the time of these injections was 11:30 P.M., and said so in my
biography of Liszt (WFL, vol. 3, p. 516). A discrepancy of fifteen minutes
may seem neither here nor there, but since Lina's observation matches exactly the time on the death certificate (which she never saw) it is more likely
than ever that the very people who were there to help Liszt dispatched him.
And all this in the presence of Cosima.

"At 11:15 the Master received 2 morphine injections in the region of the heart." Saturday, July 31, 1886.

Sunday, August 1

When I arrived home, at 4:30 A.M., I was completely frozen, and went to bed at once. I had barely rested for an hour when my landlady came in and said in all tranquility, "So Liszt is dead." This news hit me like a bullet; everything seemed to spin around in circles. I wanted to get out of bed but kept falling back in. My limbs had turned to jelly. I could not find my shoes, my skirts, and remained standing in the middle of the room uttering cries of anguish. My landlady dressed me as she saw that I was determined to go out. I wanted to run to the Master's house, but the quicker I tried to get there the longer it took. My feet would not move; it was as if they were stuck in tar. In this way I arrived at the Master's house just as Schnappauf was carrying two silver candelabras inside.[92] This was another shocking omen for me, but I still did not want to believe that he was dead.

Standing outside the front door, Miska said, "Yes, Kis-

92. Bernhard Schnappauf, the Bayreuth barber and an old factotum of Wagner's, was still in the service of Cosima. The pair of candelabras Lina saw him carrying into the house at Siegfriedstrasse were intended for the vigil over Liszt's mortal remains.

sasonge, he is dead, but you can't go in now, the Master has not been dressed yet. Come back at 10:00 A.M."

I gave him a push which he will remember and forced my way into the bedroom. He lay completely dressed on his bed, a wax-yellow color. I felt that this was how a shell looks. But the spirit was not shackled; it had joyfully freed itself and had ascended. He had a completely strange expression on his face. Yes, he looked ten years younger, very gaunt, but extraordinarily peaceful. He had not received extreme unction, but even without this he went home to Our Father with a pure heart. He had often said to me, "Pray for me when I die." Never did a prayer come so fervently from my heart than for this great deceased. Cosima sat on a sofa, across from her father. She remained seated for several minutes, then she left the room. Thus I had him alone once again, *completely* alone, and could once again press him to my heart. I took his left hand, which on Monday he had given me for hours, pressed my hand tightly in his, joined our two hands in one, and prayed together with him for the last time. Twenty minutes later Cosima returned, she took me in her arms, kissed me repeatedly, and brought me the Master's prayer book. She said that the Munkácsys would have him on their conscience, that he had still been in good health at Daniela's wedding! (She was right. It was *presumptuous* of Munkácsy to invite him to their miserable country seat after the strenuous trips to London and Paris. Whoever wanted to see Liszt should have come to *him!*) Cosima permitted me to cut off a lock of the Master's hair. I cut a thick, long lock from the root for myself. Miska came and said that I should leave, that people were coming to drape the room. Cosima told me, "But you can come back again right away." I got up and left the prayer book lying by the Master's side. She took it and said, "It belongs to you."

I went home and tidied myself up a bit and then ran into the small garden in front of my house. There I picked a bunch of forget-me-nots and ran back to the Master. I asked Cosima whether I could give them to the Master and she said, "Put them in his hand yourself." This I did, and Cosima placed the hand with the flowers on his heart. So there he lay, surrounded by the most magnificent palm trees, Wagner's bust at his head, and at his feet our Lord Jesus Christ on the Cross. The only decorations were the forget-me-nots in his small hand.

The Catholic priest arrived and held a prayer service for the family *only*. Not *one* of the three granddaughters nor Siegfried shed a single tear. Cold, without the slightest trace of melancholy, they stood around the deathbed. At 10:00 A.M. everybody received permission to view the corpse. They were allowed to linger briefly and then had to leave by the opposite door. Cosima told me to forbid the police to enter the room as long as she was inside. The grandchildren stood around both sides of the bed in a half circle. Cosima sat on his left side, at the head, her veil pulled low over her face. I stood under the cross of Christ at the foot of the bed. The public now arrived en masse. The inhabitants of Bayreuth brought along their three- and four-year-old children on their arms. Few of them were sincere in their grief. They were mostly driven by curiosity. Friedheim, Dayas, Reise-

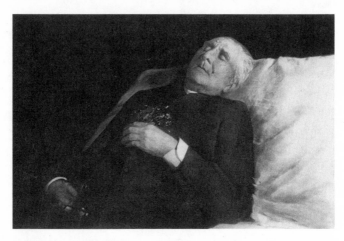

Liszt on his deathbed. His left hand is in its first position, shortly before it was moved, holding Lina Schmalhausen's forget-me-nots over his heart. Photograph by Hans Brand.

nauer,[93] and Göllerich were visibly moved. I remained standing at my place until 1:00 P.M. when everyone had to leave. I was also the last person requested to leave. A few flies were already attaching themselves to the Master's face; in addi-

93. Alfred Reisenauer (1863–1907), who has been entirely absent from Schmalhausen's narrative until now, had been a pupil of Liszt since 1876, from the age of thirteen, when he had been taken to Weimar by his parents. It was well known that Liszt did not like teaching young teenagers, but he made an exception for the youthful Prussian. Reisenauer had made his official debut in Rome, in 1881, at the home of Cardinal Gustav Hohenlohe, under Liszt's patronage, and had already started to concertize extensively. He was still a permanent part of Liszt's entourage, however, and had followed Liszt to Bayreuth in the expectation of receiving lessons there. See the photograph on p. 63.

tion there was a terrible heat made worse by the buzzing flies and masses of people. Joukowsky agreed that I should go and buy some fine muslin to protect the Master's head and hands from the flies. I bought a small bottle of pine essence as well as the fine muslin. Joukowsky and Mihalovich sent me to the Master to offer him this last service. I rubbed the essence on his head, throat and hands, then closed his left eye, which was still open, kissed him for the last time, and covered him with the muslin. Then I fetched the photographer and told him not to omit the hands from the picture. I had previously fastened three dark red roses to the Master's chest. I asked if the corpse was to be embalmed. Miska called out, "Where are we to get the money for that?" Immediately after the first photograph was taken, a plaster cast was made in the presence of Joukowsky and Mihalovich. I had rashly cut off the most beautiful front lock, which annoyed Joukowsky. In my pain I had forgotten the plaster mask, which turned out superbly, except that on both the photograph and the mask, the front lock was missing on the left side. The first photograph was not advantageous (the features had been raised and animated by the warm plaster), so we now made two others which turned out considerably better.[94] Then the barber [sic: *Barbier*] arrived. He was to

94. The photographer was Hans Brand. The two surviving photographs from the three that he took provide us with a piece of evidence that is impossible to ignore, for they conclusively support Lina's testimony. Earlier in her narrative Lina had told us that she had placed her farewell bunch of forget-me-nots in Liszt's left hand, and that Cosima in turn had placed the hand with the flowers over Liszt's heart (p. 140). And that is what the first surviving picture actually reveals. But the right hand is scarcely visible. That

embalm the body. The good fellow, of course, had never in his life embalmed a corpse and cut the whole cadaver apart. The head, as well as the body, were so bloated afterward, the face so distorted, that it was forbidden to remove the white gauze. Consequently no one was permitted to view the body during the afternoon.

Siloti, Dayas, Stavenhagen, Friedheim, Thomán, etc., hired some coaches and undertook an outing (nice, not to have to neglect the good times!)[95] In the evening they all returned

did not entirely satisfy Lina who informs us that she had instructed Hans Brand not to omit the hands. Between the taking of the second and third pictures the hands have been moved, the left one still holding the forget-me-nots and the right one holding a rosary. A comparison of the two pictures (pp. 140, 143) bears out every word of Lina's highly charged description of the events that unfolded in Liszt's death chamber during the painful hours following his death.

Incidentally, the death mask that Lina tells us was taken immediately after the first photograph was the work of the sculptor Weissbrod. It was eventually sent to Weimar and photographed by Louis Held.

95. The task of sending out telegrams to Liszt's friends and disciples, informing them of the gravity of the Master's condition, had fallen on Miska. Arthur Friedheim had left on a short trip to Leipzig a day or two before and caught the night train back to Bayreuth in the company of his mother and William Dayas. They arrived at 9:00 A.M. on August 1, where they were met at the station by Stavenhagen and Martin Krause, who informed them that Liszt was already dead. Siloti was also out of town and had returned the evening before, at dusk. He later wrote, "It was twilight, and just as I entered the street [Siegfriedstrasse] I heard the mournful howl of a dog. It proved to be Wagner's dog, who after his master's funeral had lain down beside the grave, neither howling nor moving from that time forward. The dog at the moment of Liszt's death had suddenly started howling. When I heard it I began to tremble all over" (SML, pp. 73–74).

After paying their respects at Liszt's bedside, these young men evidently went out on another trip, destination unknown. Once again we notice the resentment that Schmalhausen felt toward them. Having kept all-night vig-

Liszt on his deathbed, with Lina Schmalhausen's forget-me-nots in his left hand. The right hand holds his rosary. Photograph by Hans Brand. Beneath the picture Schmalhausen has inscribed these words: "The forget-me-nots and red roses were placed in his hands by me before the coffin was closed. No one but me garlanded the 'body' with flowers. This photograph was taken at my request. The lock of hair was taken from his left temple and handed to me by Frau Cosima Wagner at his deathbed at 6:00 o'clock in the morning, 1. 8. 86." Signed: Lina Schmalhausen.

slightly tipsy and undertook to maintain a vigil over the corpse—albeit in the adjoining room. (Cosima had locked the door to the deathroom. Inexplicably no light burned beside the deathbed during the night; the room was pitch dark.) I did not know that the young people were keeping watch, and I wanted to remain beside the corpse during the night. I knocked on the door of the house. Siloti came out, but did not admit me, and mocked me with the remark, "For ladies, entrance is forbidden." Thus the Master lay in a darkened room, without a light, and the rowdy boys next door. I went into the garden beneath his room, knelt in the sand and prayed to God for him![96]

---

ils outside Liszt's bedroom window, she now felt relegated to the status of persona non grata.

96. While the botched business of embalming Liszt's body was taking place, on Sunday, August 1, Cosima was at the Bayreuth Theatre preparing for that evening's performance of *Tristan und Isolde.* The next day, Monday, August 2, she was again at the theater for a repeat performance of *Parsifal.* Because no performances were scheduled for either August 3 or 4, Liszt's funeral was arranged for Tuesday, August 3. Schmalhausen's narrative makes clear that Cosima was at the bedside at the moment of her father's death, on the evening of July 31. A glance at the theater schedule tells us why. No performances took place that evening either. Even in death, it seems, Liszt obliged his family by dying when it was most convenient to them—a final gesture to the Bayreuth cause. Had he expired forty-eight hours earlier, or worse, forty-eight hours later, the smooth running of the festival would have been thrown into disarray.

Monday, August 2

Around nine o'clock in the morning I went into the death room once more. The Master was covered with the gauze. I wanted to look at him one more time, but the fellow (who was already cleaning the room from yesterday) asked me not to look at the corpse since it already looked too distorted. All round the deathbed stood bowls of chlorine; all the doors were open. The Master lay completely alone; no one was watching over him. The fellow scrubbed the floor and cared about nothing else. I left again and on the way I encountered a boy rolling the coffin along on a cart. It was a simple brown metal coffin. On the lid were the words "Lord Jesus Christ," in bronze. Frau Fröhlich insisted that the corpse be placed in the coffin quickly, as she had other tenants in the house. Cosima was so incensed about this that with the help of the servant Schnappauf she placed the corpse in the coffin and, picking it up by the handle, leaving the other end to her servant, she carried it herself out of the house and across the street to Wahnfried.[97] Then she sent

97. If Schmalhausen's account of these dreadful events is correct, Cosima and Schnappauf did indeed lift Liszt's rapidly decaying corpse, place it in the coffin, and carry it across the road to Wahnfried where it

her daughters into the house where he had died, had all the Master's things tossed into baskets, and had them brought to Wahnfried. (Miska was not there. He had been summoned to the Baroness von Meyendorff who had just arrived.) In the afternoon, admission to Wahnfried was forbidden. The baroness had got there in the morning and remained beside the coffin for the rest of the day. In the evening the dogs were let loose in the garden so that no uninvited persons would enter the house.

---

would "lie in state" until the funeral. Cosima must have been seething with contradictory emotions at this moment. First, the multiplicity of reactions to the unexpected death of her father; second, her manifest anger at the Fröhlichs for requesting the removal of the corpse; third, the anxious thought that in a city filled with dignitaries who had arrived from all over Europe for the Wagner festival, at least some of them might at that very moment be lingering in the vicinity of Wahnfried only to be greeted by this bizarre spectacle; and fourth, the ongoing production problems generated by *Parsifal* and *Tristan*, the solutions to which were ultimately her responsibility. It was late on Monday morning, a busy time of day in Bayreuth. And here was Cosima trundling her dead father across a street named after Wagner's operatic hero "Siegfried." A thoughtful posterity has meanwhile renamed the street "Liszt Strasse."

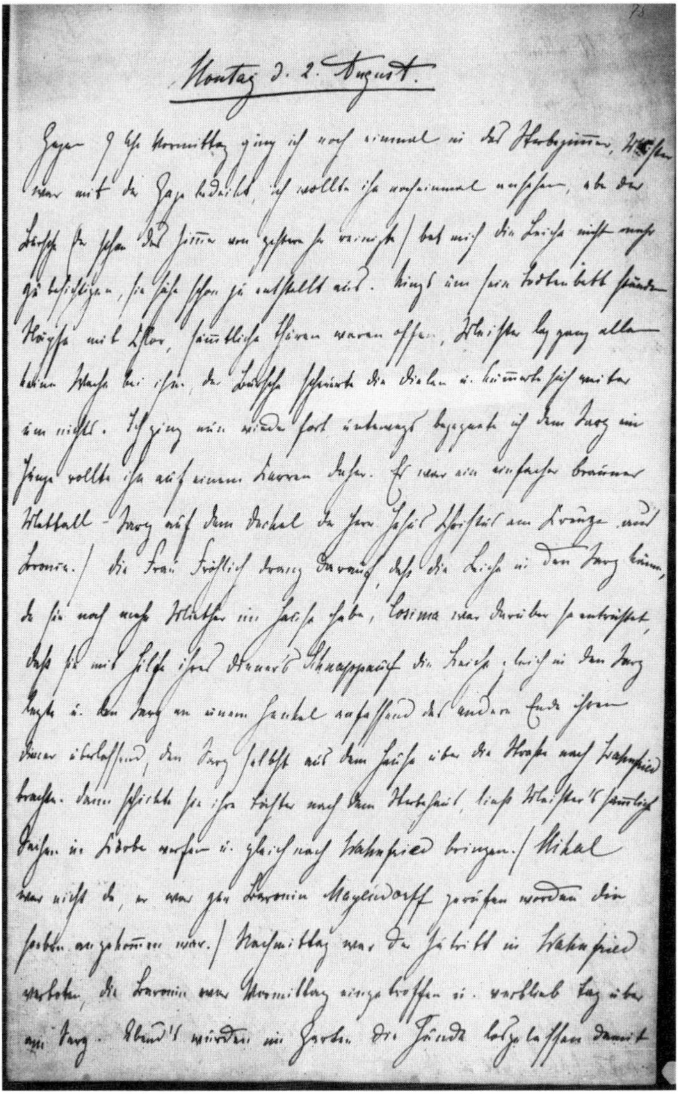

Montag d. 2. August.

[handwritten German manuscript in Kurrent script]

"I went into the death room once more." Monday, August 2, 1886.

Tuesday, August 3

At nine o'clock in the morning I went to Wahnfried to the Master's coffin and placed on it a wreath of dark-red roses that bore the inscription "Auf Wiedersehen" on the ribbon. The whole coffin was draped in mourning crepe. It stood in the middle of the front hall, surrounded by the most marvellous wreaths. Behind the head of the coffin stood the grand piano, also draped in mourning crepe. Cosima was kneeling by the coffin. I said my prayer and immediately left again so that I wouldn't have to encounter the baroness. During his lifetime the Master never wanted to see us together with him; I did not want it to happen at his coffin either. No sooner had I left than the baroness arrived.

The funeral procession was hardly dignified. There was some shoving and pushing; the funeral carriage was drawn by only four horses. Why? If Wagner's hearse could have six horses, it was certainly merited here. But in Bayreuth it was said merely that "Wagner's father-in-law has died." The name of Liszt was emphasized there very little. After the funeral I departed immediately. I had suffered enough during the past week, and each additional day spent in Bayreuth would only have increased my disgust with humanity, with his death. Only the baseness of his surroundings were left for me to enjoy. No thank you!!

I visited Bayreuth six weeks later and went to the place where the Master had died. I could hardly recognize it. The old wallpaper had been torn down and new paper put up. The floor had been waxed, there was new furniture; in short, everything was different. I was deeply hurt. They did not even have the reverence to maintain this holy room, and they had sold the deathbed with all the covers. Frau Fröhlich told me, beaming with joy, that the princess [Wittgenstein] would send her a lovely gift to repay her for the many inconveniences that the Master had caused her and for the death, which was very unpleasant for her house. She said, "I am already curious as to what she will send me. Well, you know, the old man really did cause enough inconvenience for me. And expenses as well. For where a dead person has been, everything has to be cleaned, as you can see." "By the way," she went on meekly, "I was paid for everything from over there. I received a hundred marks for the inconvenience."

That was the *true* end, the "*wretched*" end, of the great Liszt.

I went to his grave. No stone marked it. Fresh new ivy in the form of a cross was putting forth its first small leaves, surrounded by a wreath of dark blue flowers!

Epilogue

Liszt's Funeral

I

Lina Schmalhausen tells us so little about Liszt's funeral and burial service that we are left to conclude that immediately after his demise she was relegated to the sidelines and was obliged to observe what followed from a distance. Nevertheless, from a variety of other sources—including newspaper reports, correspondence, and the reminiscences of others present—it is possible to reconstruct with some accuracy the events surrounding the funeral procession, the burial service, and its difficult aftermath.

Liszt's funeral took place on Tuesday morning, August 3. At 9:00 A.M. there was a private service at Wahnfried during which the body was blessed by the town priest Father Karzendorfer. The coffin, which had been closed the previous day, was then borne out of doors and placed on a hearse drawn by four horses draped in black. At 10:00 A.M. the cortège set out on the relatively long journey down Maximilianstrasse to Bayreuth's Municipal Cemetery. Nothing had prepared Cosima for the death of her father in the middle of the Wagner festival, and the burial arrangements showed signs of improvization. The procession itself was an impressive enough spectacle, however. We are grateful that Hans Brand was able to set up his camera at a strategic point along Maximilianstrasse and capture the scene for posterity. His photograph was the only one taken of the funeral procession itself, and it formed the basis for the somewhat more detailed pencil drawing by Gérardin, which was reproduced in *Le Monde illustré* on August 21 (see p. 153).

The procession was preceded by two heralds and the Bayreuth fire brigade to marshal the crowds lining the streets. A large horse-drawn carriage headed the cortège, bearing a mass of flowers and wreaths from many countries, which had been delivered to Wahnfried and were to be laid at the graveside. Then came the coffin itself, also buried in flowers, which was borne on a carriage draped with a large black-curtained canopy and adorned with a large wreath from Crown Prince Friedrich of Germany. The four pallbearers walking alongside were Felix Mottl, Hans von Wolzogen, Baron August von Loën, and Ödön Mihalovich.[1] Immediately behind the hearse came Liszt's servants Pauline Apel and Miska who carried his master's decorations on a velvet cushion, followed by the clergy. Then came Siegfried Wagner, Henry Thode, Adolf von Gross (local banker and the leading festival administrator), and, representing the Grand Duke Carl

---

1. Two of the four pallbearers enter our narrative for the first time. Hans von Wolzogen (1848–1938) had been the editor of Wagner's propaganda sheet the *Bayreuther Blätter* ever since Wagner had founded it in February 1878. Baron August von Loën (1827–87) was the intendant of the Weimar Court Theatre.

A wood engraving of Liszt's funeral from *Le Monde illustré*, August 21, 1886, after a drawing by Gérardin, based on the photograph by Hans Brand.

Alexander, the Weimar court chamberlain Count Oskar von Wedell. Next in the procession came Liszt's students walking in two columns, bearing torches—Friedheim, Reisenauer, Felix Weingartner, Siloti, Walter Bache, Dayas, Stavenhagen, Thomán, Göllerich, and Martin Krause. Cosima had wanted to relegate them to the rear of the procession, but she relented when Friedheim and Siloti voiced their strong opposition. Then came the carriages carrying the chief mourners. In the first of them sat Cosima and her eldest daughter Daniela, together with Princess Marie von Hatzfeldt and Baroness Olga von Meyendorff, the latter of whom had arrived in Weimar the previous day to arrange to accompany Liszt to the spa of Kissingen and now found herself a mourner at his funeral. Other carriages bore various city officials, including the Mayor of Bayreuth. A large group of mourners walked at the rear. Somewhere at the back of the crowd was Anton Bruckner.

As the cortège moved slowly down Maximilianstrasse, a solemn cemetery bell could be heard tolling from the distant municipal cemetery. Black flags hung from various windows along the route. Even as the procession left Wahnfried, workmen were still hurriedly removing the multicolored bunting from the lighted gas lamps which only two days before had greeted the arrival of the crown prince (Germany's future emperor), and were replacing it with a makeshift black crepe. The funeral route was lined with visitors to the festival, many of them revelers and curiosity seekers. Walter Bache, Liszt's English pupil, who had dashed from England at twenty-four hours' notice after receiving news of Liszt's

The funeral procession of Franz Liszt, Bayreuth, August 3, 1886. Photograph by Hans Brand.

death, was still in his traveling clothes and was distressed by the levity of the crowds.[2] The procession arrived at the cemetery at 10:30 A.M., where an even larger throng of people had gathered to hear the eulogies and witness Liszt's burial. The mayor of Bayreuth, Dr. Theodor von Muncker, gave an oration and took as his theme a line from *Tristan:* "Doomed

---

2. In a letter to Jessie Laussot-Hillebrand, written after he had returned to London, Bache added that "the indifference of the musical world was fearful" (BBM, p. 308).

head, doomed heart." He did not fail to refer to Liszt as "a devoted promoter of the Wagner cause." Already that had become the politically correct thing to say in Bayreuth, with its limited view of Liszt. Eduard Reuss, a Liszt disciple, and Martin Krause then spoke. Reuss delivered a speech on behalf of the students, while Krause spoke on behalf of the recently formed Liszt society. Finally, Liszt's old friend Dr. Carl Gille came forward to deliver a farewell address, but he was so overcome with emotion that he began to weep, and his words were lost on the crowd. After Liszt's body had been lowered into the grave, Muncker placed two large laurel wreaths at the graveside, one from the city of Bayreuth and the other "from the loyal city of Vienna." Following the example of Muncker, Cosima Wagner then came forward and, together with members of the Wagner family and the Bayreuth Festival Chorus, scattered some consecrated earth over the coffin. Prominent among the floral tributes which were then piled high around the open grave was one presented on behalf of Queen Victoria by Alfred Littleton.[3] By 12:00 noon it was all over, but many people lingered to read the inscriptions on the wreaths and pay their private respects to the departed composer.

The next day a memorial service was held in the local Catholic church. A great deal of dissatisfaction was expressed

3. Alfred was the son of Henry Littleton, head of the London publishing house Novello and Company. He had helped to arrange Liszt's triumphal visit to Britain the previous April, during which time the composer had enjoyed some lavish hospitality at the family's spacious home, Westwood House, in Sydenham, Kent. Liszt had visited Queen Victoria in Windsor Castle during this final visit to Britain and had played the piano for her.

Liszt's memorial chapel, Bayreuth. Photograph c. 1900.

at the musical part of the service. It was generally thought that it would have been better to have had no music at all than to expose the distinguished audience, which included so many fine musicians, to the nasal singing of two or three priests interjecting their voices into the discordant tones of a local

Bayreuth church choir. The contrast between that and the magnificent music-making heard at the Wagner theater every night was obvious to all, and many people wondered why the festival chorus could not have participated in the service. One distinguished musician who did participate, however, was Anton Bruckner who played the organ;[4] the main selection consisted of an improvization on themes from *Parsifal*. The opportunity to perform one or two of the more important choral and organ compositions by Liszt was passed over.

II

Typical of the confusion surrounding Liszt's death were the errors in the obituary notices. The *Times* of London led the way when, in its issue of Monday, August 2, it reported

4. Anton Bruckner (1824–96) was a devoted disciple of Liszt. He had last met Liszt in Pressburg, in April 1885, bearing with him the manuscript of his newly completed Seventh Symphony, a performance of which he had wanted Liszt to arrange at the forthcoming festival of the Allgemeiner Deutscher Musikverein at Karlsruhe a few weeks later. Despite the fact that the program was already fixed, Liszt in his capacity as the president of the Musikverein prevailed upon the local organizing committee to include the massive Adagio, in which he perceived the hand of genius. The performance took place on May 30, 1885, under the direction of Felix Mottl. Bruckner was invariably overwhelmed in Liszt's presence. On this occasion he had turned up wearing a pair of large boots and buttoned leggings popular among the Austrian country folk, had removed his hat respectfully before coming into the Presence, and had addressed Liszt as: "Your Grace, Herr Canon," much to the bemusement of bystanders (SE, p. 90). The large wreath he sent to Liszt's funeral bore the inscription: "To the great master Franz Liszt."

that "Franz Liszt died last night in Bayreuth," that is, on August 1. This blunder crept into Sitwell's widely read biography of Liszt, which did duty for two generations of English readers of the story of Liszt's life. Yet more bizarre was the following sentence from the same notice: "Through a great part of his life Liszt was afflicted with a nervousness which almost amounted to hysteria, and this culminated at times in a religious melancholia nearly bordering on insanity. His friends tried several times to dissuade him from shutting himself up in a monastery"! Not to be outdone, The *New York Times* informed its readers that in his early manhood Liszt had joined Chevalier and Pereire "in their crusade against marriage and property."[5] This would have come as a total surprise to Liszt as he had joined a crusade against neither. The anonymous writers of such shoddy journalism doubtless took comfort from the fact that one of the convenient things about speaking ill of the dead is that they cannot answer back. The *Bayreuther Tagblatt,* one of the few newspapers that Wagner would allow in the house (for reasons that were apparent in nearly every issue) began its obituary notice by reminding its readers that Liszt was "the intimate friend and supporter of Wagner" and that he was "the father of Wagner's wife."[6] As the anonymous scribe warms to his theme, offering generous helpings of sympathy to Frau Cosima Wagner along the way, he reminds his readers that "all who know the great composer's true love for his relatives will feel the immensity of the loss suffered by the highly revered Wag-

5. Issue of August 1, 1886.
6. Issue of August 2, 1886.

ner family, and they may be assured, in their grief, of the most heartfelt sympathy of us all." According to this same newspaper, it had received information "from a private quarter," assuring its readers that, "Toward half past eleven that night [July 31] breathing and heartbeat ceased, and the patient passed away peacefully just as his subjective condition during the whole of his illness had been notable for its absence of any particular pain." The informant, obviously connected to the Wagner family, must have known that the last part of this sentence was a blatant untruth, put out for public consumption. The Schmalhausen diary tells a different story. The *Bayreuther Tagblatt* rounded off its article with the astonishing statement that Liszt was to be buried in the Bayreuth Municipal Cemetary "according to his own express wish." No such wish was ever uttered. As we shall presently discover, Bayreuth was already putting its own spin on the events surrounding Liszt's death, and was staking a claim to the body, even before the real struggle for its ownership had begun. In retrospect, Mayor Muncker's graveside oration takes on great significance: "[Liszt] was fated to breathe his last in the arms of his loving daughter. . . . We lay him to rest in Bayreuth's soil, just as years ago we buried our dear departed Master [i.e. Richard Wagner]. May he find it a peaceful resting place!" Worse was to follow. Within a few days of Liszt's death, Wagner's house-journal, the *Bayreuther Blätter*, came out with an obituary notice (almost certainly written by the editor Hans von Wolzogen) that began with the ominous assertion that, "A world-wanderer has returned to his

rest, and we who are left behind pray for his redemption."[7]
The writer, fresh from attending Liszt's funeral (we recall
that he had been a pallbearer in the procession) and hearing Mayor Muncker's words drawn from *Tristan*, felt constrained to pursue his own parallel between the death of
"Tristan" and the death of Liszt, by reminding "those who are
left behind" that the fulfillment of Liszt's destiny occurred
"here, in a holy place [Bayreuth!], within the circle of the
Temple of Montsalvat, where Art and Purity unite in the service of the one god above: 'Redemption by our Redeemer.'"
These pious sentiments, coming from the Bayreuth publicity
office, made everything official. Henceforth, Liszt and "Tristan" were to be inextricably linked in the Bayreuth mythol-
ogy. And by describing Bayreuth as "a holy place," the mere
idea of removing Liszt's body from the city's sacred soil became a form of sacrilege. That the Wagner family was now
working diligently behind the scenes to smooth over the
more unpleasant details of Liszt's death is borne out by the
private correspondence between Liszt's granddaughter Daniela and her father Hans von Bülow. Daniela had written to
Bülow almost at once with what were for her the essential
facts surrounding Liszt's demise. To judge from his reply,
even Bülow had been fed the party line. He wrote: "It was really, I quite agree with you, a divine dispensation that he
should have faded out painlessly at Bayreuth. All the same, in
the interests of his posthumous fame I should certainly like

7. Issue August/September, 1886, p. 245.

to see his mortal remains removed to Hungary."[8] Daniela
had visited Liszt's bedside almost daily. She knew as well as
anyone that her grandfather's end was hardly benign. Yet
here she is—true representative of the chatelaine of Bayreuth—handing out to her own father the official line that
Liszt had received a "divine dispensation to fade out painlessly" in the city of Richard Wagner—as if this was a gift for
which he should have been grateful. As to the question, Why
was not Bülow himself in attendance at Liszt's funeral? a moment's reflection will tell us why. The city was poisoned for
him through the bitter memories of Cosima's adulterous relationship with Wagner during the final years of her doomed
marriage to Bülow himself, of her elopement with Wagner,
and of his certain (if secret) knowledge that his third daughter, Isolde von Bülow, was actually sired by Wagner. Bülow
had never stepped foot in Bayreuth since it had become a
Wagner shrine. In all things pertaining to this city Bülow re-
lied increasingly on whatever news his eldest daughter
Daniela was able to give him about it.

More grotesque still was the obituary notice that was
printed in the *Coburger Tageblatt,* which began with the sin-
gular statement: "Liszt died on October 11, 1811, in Raiding,
in the district of Oedenburg,"[9] thus depriving him of his entire life plus eleven days—a typographical error which, if
one bears in mind the intense rivalry already evident between the Liszt and Wagner factions, reads like an uncon-

8. Letter dated "Meiningen, September 9, 1886." See GLB, p. 377.

9. Issue of August 1, 1886: "Liszt wurde den 11. Oktober1811 in Raiding
bei Oedenburg gestorben."

scious death wish of Freudian proportions. The French journal *Le Monde illustré*[10] beneath its picture of Liszt's funeral, blithely informed its readers that he was buried on August 4—that is, one day late—as if to stay in line with the *Times,* which had him die on August 1, one day later than his actual demise.[11]

Of the many obituary notices that appeared in North America, one of the most audacious was surely that of *The American Art Journal.*[12] After archly advising its readers that "all the newspaper [reports] . . . were considerably spoiled by the literal reproduction of many facts and judgments implying a common source of information," the journal found a source of information all its own by moving into the realm of dreams and fantasies. It informed us that the true reason that Liszt had entered Holy Orders in 1865 was that the mother of his three children, the Countess Marie d'Agoult, "of whose character we prefer not to speak," had deserted him suddenly. Two married ladies to whom he had earlier promised marriage if they ever became free now emerged from his past. They "did indeed obtain their freedom on the same day, the one by her husband's death, the other by divorce." Not knowing how to escape the dilemma in which he

10. Issue of August 21, 1886.

11. For the rest, it has to be observed that from the start Liszt was singularly unfortunate in his obituaries. We recall that when he was only seventeen years old, a false obituary notice had been published in the Paris newspaper *Le Corsaire,* which began with the sensational and completely false sentence: "The young Liszt has died in Paris" (issue of October 23, 1828). At the time of his supposed "demise," Liszt was at home, quietly celebrating his seventeenth birthday.

12. Issue of August 7, 1886, p. 5.

now found himself, the readers of the *Art Journal* were asked to believe that Liszt accepted the advice of his friend Cardinal Hohenlohe and escaped into the priesthood. Silliness could go no further. Liszt and the Countess d'Agoult had separated in 1844; Liszt took Holy Orders in 1865, twenty-one years later; he never "entered the priesthood," and because he never rose to the level of Sub-Deacon in the hierarchy of the church (which is the first of the Sacramental Orders), he was free to marry.

Even the English dominions beyond the seas felt constrained to express an opinion about Liszt. Under the pious title "A Lesson from Liszt," *The Spectator*,[13] a widely read newspaper in Upper Canada, came out with an obituary notice that pointed out to its largely Protestant readership that Liszt had been corrupted by city life, and that the lack of any vast moral elevation prevented him from composing well. The "lesson" in question was that "those who have left posterity the richest legacy . . . [were those who] bore the white flowers of a blameless life." And lest the point be lost on his flock, the good shepherd rushed to provide two examples of lily-white morality: "The sunny sweetness and purity of Mendelssohn" and the "chaste majesty of Beethoven." Queen Victoria was clearly alive and well, and the rustle of her virtuous skirts was to be heard throughout her empire.

As late as 1911, the one-hundredth anniversary of Liszt's birth, those critics who had every reason to know better were still romanticizing his death. The American Lisztian James Huneker wrote: "On July 31 Liszt died, what to him must

13. Issue of August 4, 1886.

have been a pleasant death, after witnessing the greatest work of the poet-composer whom he had done so much to befriend—Richard Wagner's *Tristan und Isolde.*"[14] And in 1936, the fiftieth anniversary of Liszt's death, those who had been members of his circle were still proving themselves incapable of coming to grips with the precise date of his demise. His pupil Frederick Riesberg, in an otherwise interesting essay marking this memorial year, informed his readers that Liszt went "serenely to his sleep," on July 21, 1886.[15] Liszt's end would indeed have been serene had it occurred on the date given. But it was the ten days that followed that made the difference, and which gave the raison d'être for the Schmalhausen diary.

Whatever her outward composure, Cosima was thrown into turmoil by the death of her father. But she could not allow herself to show it. The day after his death she had gone straight to the theater in order to supervise that evening's performance of *Tristan*. Liszt's body had been locked in the darkened death room at Siegfriedstrasse throughout the entire performance—an image on whose symbolism it does not do to dwell. And on August 2 she had supervised the arrangements for *Parsifal* as well. She could have done nothing less, since it would have been impossible to cancel this international event which had attracted a large contingent of distinguished visitors to the festival. For the next few weeks Cosima found herself in the middle of some serious disputes with the grand duke of Weimar and with the Hun-

14. *Franz Liszt*, New York, 1911, p. 280.
15. "Gala Days with Liszt at Weimar," *Etude*, November 1936, p.738.

garian government regarding her father's last resting place. Although these wrangles have already been touched on in the prologue, we need to return to them here if we are fully to understand the extraordinary set of complications that gathered around the competing claims for Liszt's remains. It is a little-known aspect of his posthumous fate and perhaps the strangest one of all.

III

Liszt himself must be held partly responsible for the dispute because he left no instructions for the disposition of his body in his will (1861).[16] Moreover, at various times and in various places, he had expressed contradictory wishes on the subject of his grave. In 1863 he had mentioned Rome as a place of interment. In 1866 he told his son-in-law Emile Ollivier that he would like to be buried in St. Tropez, near his deceased daughter Blandine. Later still, he told Cardinal Gustav Hohenlohe that he would like to be buried in Tivoli, a place in his final years where he had enjoyed peaceful seclusion at the Villa d'Este. To add to the confusion, Ödön

16. That fact became evident when a copy of the document was dispatched from Weimar to Bayreuth. The only reference Liszt made to the disposition of his body in his will was that he wanted "to be buried simply, without any pomp whatsoever, and if possible at night." These wishes were not carried out. One piece of information it did contain, however, and which must have caused Cosima heartburn, was to name Princess Carolyne von Sayn-Wittgenstein, his companion of nearly forty years, as his "residual legatee." In brief, Carolyne was his executrix, and she now emerged with full legal powers to execute his will.

Mihalovich and Count Apponyi, two of Liszt's distinguished compatriots, came forward after the funeral insisting that Liszt had told them many times that he wanted to be buried in Hungary. In 1869, however, Liszt had been affronted by the ostentatious funeral of the painter Johann Overbeck, and had written to Princess Carolyne that he wanted no such funeral for himself: "Let my body be buried, not in a church, but in some cemetery, and let it not be removed from that grave to any other. I will not have any other place for my body than the cemetery which is in use in the place where I die."[17]

Although this crucial letter was not published until many years after his death, and although its contents were completely unknown to Cosima at the time and to practically everybody else, it contained one sentiment that must have been vouchsafed to Miska the manservant, because within hours of Liszt's death, he had told Cosima that it was Liszt's wish to be buried where he fell.[18] This was music to Cosima's ears because it bolstered her desire to keep her father's body in Bayreuth. Useless to argue that the letter had been written in 1869, seventeen years earlier; that the Bayreuth Festival did not yet exist; that the marriage of Wagner to Cosima had not yet taken place; that his relations with Cosima had since entered a precipitous decline; that in 1869 he could have had no inkling that he would die in such wretched circumstances, in a rented room of a boardinghouse located in

17. November 27, 1869. LLB, vol. 6, pp. 228–29.

18. This is what Cosima herself tells the grand duke of Weimar in her letter to him p. 170. Liszt's original disclosure to Princess Carolyne (1869) was later leaked to the *Leipziger Tageblatt*, which published fragments of the letter on December 6, 1888.

what had meanwhile become the city of Wagner. Useless, too, to point out that a letter is not a will, and that it is no more binding on the people who read it than if its contents had been delivered during an impromptu conversation over dinner. The only phrase that mattered was "to be buried where he fell," and it became impossible to dislodge.

Meanwhile, there was an interesting suggestion that the remains should be transferred to Eisenach and laid to rest at the foot of the Wartburg in the Elisabeth Church, because of its deep connections to Hungary's national saint who had lived in the Wartburg and whose tragic life had inspired Liszt's oratorio *Saint Elisabeth,* a work that had received its premiere there. Liszt's natal village of Raiding, too, wanted its famous son returned to the place of his birth; the village elders were still pressing this matter as late as 1906. Both these cases had merit, and in the popular imagination either location would have made a satisfying ending to the colorful journey of Liszt's life.

But Weimar and Budapest had stronger claims. Within days of Liszt's death, in fact, the Hungarian press was in a tumult about the funeral arrangements. In its issue of August 5, 1886, the *Neue Freie Presse* spoke for everybody when it stated that it would be an "insult to educated Europe" if Hungary left its greatest son lying on foreign soil. Princess Carolyne supported the claim of the Franciscan monastery in Pest to have Liszt returned there, and she enlisted the help of Liszt's Viennese lawyer Dr. Johann Brichta to help her achieve this end. As a member of the Order of Saint Francis, and as someone who had kept in regular touch with this particular monastery since his childhood, it would have been an entirely appropriate resting place for Liszt.[19] It appears that Carolyne had forgotten about the letter Liszt had written to her in 1869 telling her that he wished to be buried where he fell. When many years later her daughter, Princess Marie Hohenlohe, was asked about that, she replied, "I believe that in her great grief, and already very ill, she no longer remembered this letter which I found among her papers."[20] Moreover, Carolyne had staunch allies. Ödön Mihalovich was adamant that Liszt had told him many times that he wanted to be buried in Hungary. The Hungarian government began to show some interest, and informal contacts were made with Cosima Wagner as a result of which she made it known that she would seriously consider allowing her father's body to be transferred to Budapest if the request came from the Hungarian government itself. A full-blown debate on this matter took place in the House of Representatives on February 26, 1887.[21] While there was general support for the idea of bringing Liszt home, it foundered on the shoals of local politics. A short time earlier the legislature had debated the return of

19. Although the monastery no longer exists, the Franciscan church that used to adjoin it still stands on its original site at the corner of Kossuth and Károlyi Mihály streets. Liszt often dined at the monastery, knew many of the monks by name, and frequently raised money for them. He continued to worship at the church whenever he visited Budapest, until the last year of his life.

20. Letter to Count Géza Zichy, dated September 25, 1911 (PHZ, p. 292).

21. The debate is reported in full in the *Proceedings of the House of Representatives, 1884–1887*, 332nd sitting, volume 16, February 26, 1887. I have provided a detailed summary of the text in the third volume of my biography of Liszt (WFL, vol. 3, pp. 524–25).

the body of Prince Ferenc Rákózcy II, the national warrior who had taken up arms against the Turkish invaders of his country and whose body had been buried on Turkish soil for 150 years. During the debate, the distinguished Hungarian historian Kálmán von Thaly reminded the House that a petition from fifty Hungarian municipalities urging the return of Rákózcy was still before the Committee of the Interior, mired in bureaucracy. It would be an insult to Rákózcy's memory, Thaly argued, if Liszt was returned to Hungary before Rákózcy himself. All Liszt had done was to transcribe the march named for the man who really did deserve a national homecoming! Matters were not helped when the prime minister of the day, Kálmán Tisza, made a speech in which he criticized Liszt's book *The Gypsies and Their Music in Hungary* for making a gift of Magyar music to the Gypsies. Liszt had his defenders during the debate, of course, and there was a powerful speech in his behalf from his old friend and colleague Kornél Ábrányi (the secretary of the Royal Academy of Music), but it failed to carry the day. Cosima followed this debate with care. Almost from the start, she knew that the arguments coming out of Hungary would be borne away on the wind. The formal request from the Hungarian government that she was seeking would never materialize.

IV

It was the claim of Weimar that gave Cosima the most trouble. An important run of unpublished letters between

Cosima and the Grand Duke Carl Alexander of Weimar throws essential light on the entire affair.[22] Carl Alexander had looked on with growing concern as news of Liszt's burial in Bayreuth, and the dispute now swirling around it, reached him. As early as October 14, 1886, the monarch had written to Cosima asking her to permit the bringing of Liszt's remains to Weimar. He had observed Hungary's growing interest and hastened to intervene. He told her that if Budapest wanted the body transferred to Hungary, then Weimar had an even stronger claim. Cosima's reply was deliberately vague. She asked Carl Alexander to consider the difficulty of her present situation with regard to various problems arising out of her dealings with Dr. Johann Brichta (the Viennese lawyer briefed by Princess Carolyne) and she enclosed copies of her correspondence with Brichta, as well as a letter from Mayor Theodor Muncker.

On October 22, Liszt's birthday, Carl Alexander sent a crucial reply to Cosima, repeating his wish to have Liszt's remains transferred to Weimar, offering to build her father a mausoleum worthy of his memory and enclosing a letter from Carl Gille, who now confirmed in writing that Liszt had many times expressed the wish to be buried in Weimar.

Cosima replied the following day, turning down this offer. Her remarkable letter has never before been published and we give it here in full:

22. It may be found in the Hausarchiv Carl Alexander, Abt. A XXVI, no. 1182: "The correspondence of Carl Alexander and Cosima Wagner in 1886."

Bayreuth, 23 October 1886

Your Grace:

I beg your Royal Highness to accept my gratitude for the kind attention you have paid to my words and for the communication of Dr. Gille's letter. Would you allow me, Sire, to submit to you my objections to the contents of this letter.

I find it difficult to believe that a conversation on such a delicate matter as the death of one of the parties could have been held with such freedom and frankness. It is certainly true that my father feared neither thinking nor speaking of death; but I am absolutely convinced that his innate excessive tact would have made him greet with a slightly ironical smile the prospect of preceding his friend to the grave.

Therefore I do not believe that the conversation took place in the way in which Mons. Gille reports it to us, but that what almost always happens in such cases happened to him; that is, he thought he had said what he himself was thinking, and he thought that he had heard what corresponded to his own wishes. How can one explain otherwise the contradiction between the sensible wishes expressed by my father? As for her, the sole executrix[23] is perfectly sure that my father expressed to her on several occasions the wish to be buried at the Franciscans convent in Pest. I cannot prevent myself from believing yet again in this instance in one of those mirages of the imagination that are so natural and common and which mislead even people of the best of intentions. As

23. Cosima cannot even bring herself to write the name of Princess Carolyne but refers to Liszt's companion of nearly forty years as "her, the sole executrix." It is amusing to note that Carolyne had a similar aversion to using Cosima's name and referred to her in the letter from which we quote on p. 177 as "she who for three years would not see her own father."

for me, I have more faith in the report of the manservant; first, because he had no personal motive, either sentimental or otherwise, for doing as he did; second, because he put the question to my father for practical reasons with the aim of clearing up in his mind and getting guidance in a difficult situation for himself. This my father certainly understood and certainly approved of the precaution, and answered him not in general terms that the dead should not be transported, but very personally that he intended to rest in the place where he fell asleep. That answer conforms so well to what I know about my father's sentiments relating to our mortal coil that I am convinced of its authenticity. I am also convinced that my father felt his end approaching and that if the thought of reposing here near his family had not seemed pleasant to him he would have spoken to me about his last resting place.

It remains only to speak of the honor! And it is a very great one, Sire, and which I am far from not knowing how to recognize, the one you are doing him by assigning him his sepulcher on the land that was the cradle and shelter of the greatest heroes of action and thought and where he himself spent the most fruitful years of his life and sowed the seed for what was one day to blossom in Bayreuth.

Your Grace will be good enough to understand that I am not free and will allow me to express my gratitude for his benevolent remembrance on the consecrated day and to ever call myself

Your Royal Highness's very humble servant

C. Wagner

Several things strike us about this extraordinary reply, and they are worth dwelling on. Cosima's naive belief that her father would have told her if he had not found the idea of resting in the bosom of his family pleasant to him would be comical if it were not so preposterous. If the Schmalhausen diary teaches us anything at all, it is that Bayreuth and the Wagner family were slowly becoming anathema to him. He had never wanted to visit the place during that fatal summer of 1886, but the wedding of his granddaughter Daniela, which provided the opportunity for Cosima herself to make a special request that he attend the festival, had given him little choice in the matter. This city was the one place, unlike any other, where he said that he did *not* want to die, and he said it several times. Her dismissal of Gille's letter, too, is arrogant, for we know from countless other sources that Liszt had often considered Weimar as a last resting place, and it would have been a perfectly natural thing for him to have mentioned that fact to Gille, his close friend of many years standing. His will (1861) had been written and registered in Weimar, and he had had a home there for almost forty years—save for an interruption in the 1860s. As for Cosima's perfumed reply to the grand duke that the offer to have her father's remains transferred to Weimar was honor enough, so the honor of *actually* transferring them was unnecessary, it ranks as a euphemism worthy of a professional diplomat. Finally, there is the telltale sentence that it was in Weimar that Liszt sowed the seeds of the blossoms that appeared only later in Bayreuth. Anyone interested in the finer points of historiography, and the way in which the details can be manipulated to suit a particular end, will have no difficulty in recognizing the signal that Cosima was sending to the world while her father was still warm in the grave. Wagner was the "blossom"; Liszt had merely "sown the seeds."

And this brings us to the nub of the matter. Cosima never had any intention of letting her father's remains leave Bayreuth if she could possibly prevent it. Her chief motive in wanting her father buried there was, so to speak, to keep him as a trophy for future festivals. Within days of his death, this speculation was rampant among Liszt's friends and disciples. His American pupil William Dayas summed up the sentiments of many when he wrote from Bayreuth to his sister Emma: "On Tuesday morning he was buried—in the common graveyard—among common people—and that by his daughter. Why? Because it would ruin the opera business in Bayreuth to make as much of Liszt her father as of Wagner her husband. It was sad."[24] By the same token, Dayas is implying, it would help "the opera business in Bayreuth" to make less of Liszt her father than of Wagner her husband, and the simplest way to ensure that would be to keep the body in Bayreuth under Wagner's shadow.

V

Even while the negotiations over her father's remains were in progress, both with Hungary and with Weimar, it is evident

24. WDC, unpublished.

that Cosima was engaged in an enormous bluff. We can say this with some certainty because of the little matter of the memorial chapel beneath which Liszt's remains still repose. On October 25, while she was in correspondence with the grand duke, and only three days after the monarch's generous offer was made, Cosima announced a competition for the design of a permanent memorial chapel to contain Liszt's burial plot in the Bayreuth cemetery. It effectively trumped the grand duke's offer from Weimar. The project must have been on her mind for several weeks at least. Certainly her plan was far advanced by the time she replied to the grand duke on October 23, but she was careful to conceal it from him.

The commission went to the Munich architect Gabriel Seidl who obligingly incorporated some features of a design already worked out by the seventeen-year-old Siegfried Wagner, whose lively interest in architecture (which he later studied professionally) had already manifested itself. By September 1887 the structure was in place. Over the portal of the chapel ran the words: "I know that my Redeemer liveth." From the beginning, the design of the memorial chapel had many critics among Liszt's supporters who thought it cramped and in poor taste. In the closing days of World War II an American artillery shell obliged them by hitting the chapel and doing much damage; almost at the same time an American warplane dropped a bomb on Wahnfried necessitating extensive repairs. Liszt's coffin was exhumed and reburied on the same site, beneath a simple marble slab. In 1978 the city of Bayreuth, that had meanwhile come to appreciate the presence of Liszt in its midst, if only as a tourist attraction, rebuilt the original mausoleum over his grave, which still stands today.

Liszt's posthumous fate would have been quite different if his two other children, Blandine and Daniel, had remained alive. Their father's body would surely have been removed from Bayreuth with dispatch. From what we know of their strong attachment to Liszt, Cosima's opinion would not have carried much weight, given all the difficulties with which she was now beleaguered in Bayreuth. But Blandine had died shortly after giving birth to her first child, in 1862, while Daniel (who had trained for the law in Vienna) had died in 1859, aged twenty. Similar opposition to Cosima could have been mounted by Liszt's cousin Eduard Liszt, a brilliant lawyer who had risen to become the royal imperial prosecutor in Vienna, the highest legal position in the Austro-Hungarian Empire. For many years Eduard had looked after Liszt's legal affairs and had even handled the investment portfolios of both Liszt and Princess Carolyne. But Eduard had died in 1879 and with him the possibility of reason prevailing over the emotional obstacles that Cosima was always placing along the path to her father's final resting place.

The quarter century that followed saw a gradual shift in Liszt's posthumous reputation, not only in Bayreuth but throughout the musical world. In 1887 his vast correspondence with Wagner was published, which offered proof positive of Liszt's generosity toward him, especially during the years of exile.[25] The letters revealed, among other things,

25. *Briefwechsel zwischen Wagner und Liszt,* 2 vols. (Leipzig, 1887). They were translated into English by Francis Hueffer and published in London

the vital role that Liszt had played in helping to procure a pardon for Wagner, the substantial gifts of money he had made to the impoverished composer across the years, and the help that he had later extended toward the Bayreuth Festival itself. These trifling matters the Wagner family would doubtless have preferred to hush up. It is a little-known fact in the family drama that after Wagner's death, in 1883, Cosima had exerted pressure on Liszt to have all Wagner's letters to her father returned to her. She used her daughter Daniela as a go-between, not wishing to tackle Liszt directly on so delicate a matter. It was an audacious request, and Liszt refused to grant it, a fact for which we remain grateful, because had Cosima procured these letters, many of them would never have seen the light of day or worse, would have been tailored to reflect the Bayreuth perspective.

Meanwhile, what of Princess Carolyne, who for years had lived a reclusive life in Rome? When she learned of Liszt's death from the newspapers, she took to her bed and never left it. She suffered a stroke[26] that incapacitated her but she was kept closely informed of the funeral arrangements by her faithful correspondent Adelheid von Schorn, who, as we learn from Schmalhausen's diary, was an almost daily visitor at Liszt's bedside. Even had she been fit enough to travel, however, it is doubtful that Carolyne would have set foot in

---

the following year. In 1910 Erich Kloss brought out a second, expanded edition. See BWL and KWL.

26. The first mention of this "seizure," as she termed it, was to La Mara [Marie Lipsius] in a letter dated "Rome, December 10, 1886." See LDML., vol. 2, pp. 136–37.

Bayreuth. A mutual repugnance had long ago sprung up between Carolyne and Cosima, which can be traced back to
Cosima's elopement with Wagner and her subsequent divorce from Hans von Bülow, in July 1870, a drama that had
torn Liszt himself asunder. Carolyne was later to describe the
emotional upheaval of this divorce to Lina Ramann: "I went
through the death of his son with him, as well as those of his
daughter Blandine and of his mother—but nothing that can
be compared with this despair."[27] Cosima rightly accused
Carolyne of waging a long campaign of intrigue against her
and Wagner and of trying to turn Liszt against them and the
Bayreuth enterprise. Carolyne was aghast that Liszt had died
in "pagan Bayreuth," and her strong Catholic sentiments
were deeply perturbed when she learned that he was to be
buried in a Protestant churchyard, among a "nest of athe-
ists." Almost as troubling to her was the fact that Liszt's funeral had been completely overshadowed by the Wagner
festivities. Enraged, she put pen to paper and wrote a letter
that gave vent to her bitter feelings:

> I sent for the Bayreuth newspapers from July 28 to August
> 10. Just think—*not once* is Liszt's illness mentioned, as in a
> bathing resort where illness and death are hushed up in or-
> der to arouse no painful sensitivities among the bathers.
> I send you the paper of August 2 in which his death is
> then announced straight away. Then, the fact that he was a
> Catholic is kept quiet, or kept dark. Every reader will think
> that he was buried in this nest of atheists by some free-
> thinking Protestant clergyman! In the issue of August 11

27. RL, p. 76.

you can see that she who for three years would not see her
own father [after Wagner's death] was staying ten days later
in the public house called "The Gaiety" [*Zum Frohsinn*]. On
both the last two evenings she was in the theater, for the
show must go on, and Cosima was so fond of playing the
producer that she remained there day and night.[28]

Carolyne died on March 9, 1887. She went to her grave
protesting against Liszt's burial site in Bayreuth. With her
death, however, the last legal challenge confronting the
chatelaine of Bayreuth was removed. The desire on the part
of the rest of the world to have Liszt's body removed from
Bayreuth remained very much alive, however. One file in the
Weimar archives contains newspaper clippings on the topic
that cover a span of forty years.[29] But all such discussions
foundered on one simple fact. Cosima survived until 1930,
outliving the opposition, and all attempts to reverse her fait
accompli came to naught.

VI

Once the struggle for her father's body had been won,
Cosima embarked on the much more difficult task of gain-

28. KFL, rev. ed., p. 297. Julius Kapp does not tell us to whom this dramatic letter was addressed. In 1924, when it was first published, Cosima was
still alive, and we surmise that he desired to shield the identity of the recip-
ient. Carolyne's chief correspondent on all matters concerning Liszt's personal life was her old friend from Weimar, Adelheid von Schorn, who had
been present at the funeral.

29. GSA, 270/4.

ing control over his biography as well. We have already mentioned that she was thwarted in her attempt to get possession of the Liszt-Wagner correspondence, in 1883, a major setback for her. Although it was not known at the time of Liszt's death, she already possessed a very large archive of Liszt materials, including a vast correspondence of more than a thousand letters between Liszt and his three children, between Liszt and his mother, and between the children and their grandmother, Anna Liszt. This irreplaceable material had come into Cosima's possession with the deaths of her brother and sister. There were also invaluable documents such as the diary of the 15-year-old Liszt and a precious cache of photographs, all of which would have been of inestimable value to his biographers. For nearly ninety years this material remained in the personal possession of the Wagner family, hidden from public view. Few if any Liszt biographers knew of the existence of a Liszt archive in Bayreuth, and while Cosima was alive not a single biographer gained access to it. After Cosima's death, in 1930, this policy of "private ownership" remained in force. It was not until 1974 that the Wagner archives passed into the possession of the city of Bayreuth and with them the Bayreuth-based Liszt materials as well. That Cosima harbored a desire to project an image of her father as a "good Wagnerian" cannot be doubted. Her book *Franz Liszt: Ein Gedenkblatt von seiner Tochter* was published in 1911, the one-hundredth anniversary of his birth. She devoted several pages to the princess, to the latter's relationship to Liszt, to their thwarted marriage, and to the attachment that both of them had to the Roman Catholic church, although she was an authority on none of these matters. Her dislike of Carolyne led her to produce distortions. She had already made it known that her father looked forward to his marriage to the princess "as to a burial service."[30] We need look no further than the mutilated version of Liszt's will that she published as a supplement to her book to see malevolence at work. All references to Carolyne have been expunged. To show the extent of the damage, they are restored in the following passages, within brackets:

> And now I kneel once more [with Carolyne] to pray [as we have often done together] that the reign of our Father Who is in Heaven may come, that His Will be done on earth as it is in Heaven. Forgive us our trespasses as we forgive them that trespass against us and deliver us from evil. Amen!
>
> Written on September 14, the Festival of the Exaltation of the Holy Cross [in the absence of Carolyne, who left here for Rome on May 17 last]
>
> I wish to be buried simply, without any pomp whatsoever, and if possible at night. May eternal light shine on my soul. [My last breath will be a blessing for Carolyne.]
> F. Liszt.

These and many other cuts represent a serious suppression of the historical record. Cosima must have known that she was simply reproducing a truncated version of the will, previously published in the *Neue Zeitschrift für Musik* on 4 May 1887, nine months after Liszt's death. The unexpurgated text

30. *Bayreuther Blätter,* March 1900, p. 82.

of the will had already been published by La Mara in 1900,[31] eleven years before the appearance of Cosima's own *Gedenk-blatt*. This definitive text of Liszt's will contains many flattering references to Carolyne—"whom I have so dearly wished to call by the sweet name of wife"—the sort of sentence that must have had an apoplectic effect on her nemesis Cosima.

VII

To anyone interested in the way in which biography comes to be written, and in the subtle influences that can be brought to bear on the narrative so that it reflects one interpretation rather than another, Liszt's death in Bayreuth offers a rich field for study. From Cosima's telling phrase "Liszt sowed the seed for what was one day to blossom in Bayreuth," an entire history of her father's biography may be inferred, to say nothing of that of her husband. The opponents and proponents of such a view were already lined up behind Liszt's coffin, even as the funeral cortège was setting out for the Bayreuth cemetery. Henceforth it would be de rigueur for generations of biographers with sympathy toward Liszt and his music to include plenty of ballast whose chief function was to weight the narrative against Wagner. One need read no further than the chapter "Wagner Aggrieved" in William Wallace's perceptive book *Liszt, Wagner, and the Princess* (1927), to witness how this bias worked

31. LLB, vol. 5, pp. 52–63.

against Wagner. By the same token, to revere Wagner was to revile Liszt. The chief example was Ernest Newman's character assassination of Liszt in his book *The Man Liszt* (1934), which arose directly from work he was doing on the second volume of his monumental biography of Richard Wagner. The pejorative language used by Newman is at times astounding. Few doubt that if Newman had never written his magnum opus he would have lacked the incentive to divest himself of such negative opinions about Liszt. In earlier years he had been well enough disposed toward him.[32]

Once the biographers sensed the way that things were moving, it became necessary to include in any biography of Liszt a table of music examples showing how he had anticipated some of Wagner's leading themes by many years. With enthusiasm bordering on joy, supporters of Liszt have pointed to themes from *Die Walküre, Parsifal,* and *Tristan* that appeared to have started life in Liszt's "Faust" Symphony, in his choral work *Excelsior!,* and in his song "Ich möchte hingehn" respectively.[33] As early as 1911, the one-hundredth anniversary of Liszt's birth, the artist Georges Villa depicted Liszt in a cartoon, which has meanwhile become famous, as a kind of Merlin breaking open an egg with his baton (or

32. See, for example, Newman's highly positive remarks about Liszt in his essay "Faust in Music" (NMS, pp. 93–94). Newman's widow has told us that his opinion of Liszt began to change while he was still struggling to complete the second volume of his life of Wagner (NEN, p. 124).

33. I include myself in this review and refer in particular to my essay "Liszt's Musical Background," in my symposium "Franz Liszt: The Man and His Music" (pp. 70–73) written nearly thirty-five years ago. In those days, the "echo effect" was somewhat more pronounced than it is today.

was it a magic wand?), bringing forth the fledgling Wagner within. He called his sketch "Liszt precursor of Wagner." The title summed up the growing sentiment of a new generation. And it was the exact opposite of everything that Bayreuth had been saying.

Bayreuth responded that same year. It is often forgotten, even by the aficionados, that during the Liszt centenary celebrations of 1911, when there was a European-wide attempt to bring the composer's life and work into much sharper focus than hitherto, with Liszt concerts in most of the major capitals, Cosima Wagner thought the moment ripe to publish Wagner's autobiography, *Mein Leben*. It was as if she felt compelled to force the attention of the world away from her father during his anniversary year and back once more to Wagner. And *Mein Leben* was an extraordinary book, which changed the direction of his biography. Wagner had dictated the story of his life to Cosima over a period of years, not really knowing whether the book would ever be published. But Cosima, who was now seventy-four-years old, was determined to bring it out during her own lifetime, and her timing could not have been more opportune as far as the Bayreuth cause was concerned. Although the book contains some important references to Liszt, he is (not unnaturally) presented in a subservient light to Wagner himself.

Cosima knew that an even more substantial work was waiting in the wings to support the Bayreuth cause, and that was her own diaries. In these remarkable volumes she shows her strong ambivalence toward her father. She also records a number of highly damaging comments about Liszt that Wagner had uttered in private, most famously his depiction of Liszt's later music as "budding insanity." Cosima had penned that phrase on November 29, 1882,[34] less than four years before her father's death. She would not have known at that time that such a sentiment placed Wagner in an impossible contradiction. It was not until 1887 that she would have been able to read for the first time Wagner's earlier panegyric to Liszt: "I think that I have discovered that you are the greatest musician of all time."[35] Both statements cannot be true.

In fact, the polarity that emerged in the field of Liszt-Wagner biographies goes back much earlier than Cosima's letter to the grand duke, and a striking antecedent can be mentioned here. Hans von Bülow, Liszt's favorite pupil and former son-in-law, the first husband of Cosima, had stood in awe of Liszt in the early days, had championed his music in the press, had defended it in fiery speeches from the podium, and had given the world premieres of Liszt's B minor piano sonata (1857) and his *Totentanz* for piano and orchestra (1865). But by the early 1870s his opinion had begun to change. After he had started to conduct the works of Richard Wagner with regularity (he had directed the first performance of *Tristan* in Munich in 1865), he stopped conducting Liszt altogether. When Liszt dedicated his "Goethe March" to Bülow and the Meiningen Orchestra, Bülow described it as "an unparalleled scar on the face." What makes the Bülow case so noteworthy is that at the time of his painful divorce from Cosima, it was Wagner who had treated him

34. WT, vol. 2, p. 1059.
35. BWL, vol. 2, p. 143.

with near contempt and Liszt who had supported him and fought for him. He suffered a nervous breakdown as a result of this personal trauma and attempted suicide. Under all the normal conditions governing human relations Bülow would have remained steadfast to Liszt for the rest of his life. But the pull of Wagner's music was irresistible, and the only way that Bülow could make room for it, evidently, was by jettisoning the music of Liszt. Interestingly, he did not jettison the music of Mendelssohn, Schumann, or Brahms, composers with whom he also had a lifelong affinity.

As for Wagner's side of the equation, it is more interesting still. It, too, predated Cosima's letter to the grand duke by a good many years. In July 1856, after a careful study of the orchestral scores of Liszt's symphonic poems, Wagner admitted that his style of composition had undergone a radical change for which Liszt was entirely responsible. He confessed to Liszt:

> Every day I read one or another of your scores, just as I would read a poem, easily and without hindrance. Then I feel every time as if I had dived into a crystalline flood, there to be quite by myself, having left all the world behind, to live for an hour my own proper life. Refreshed and invigorated, I then come to the surface again, full of longing for your personal presence.[36]

Although this confession was well known within Lisztian circles, it was whispered in undertones, as if one were not supposed to mention such things aloud. But in 1859, one of

36. Letter dated July 20, 1856. KWL, vol. 2, p. 130.

Liszt's disciples, the critic Richard Pohl, finally broke the silence by writing a series of articles in the *Neue Zeitschrift für Musik* in which he traced the influence of the newly composed *Tristan* Prelude directly to Liszt.[37] This caused consternation on Wagner's side, and he wrote to Bülow:

> It is hinted that since my acquaintance with Liszt's compositions I have become quite a different fellow in harmony from what I was before. But when friend Pohl blurts out this secret before the whole world, at the very head of a short analysis of the *Tristan* Prelude, this is, to say the least, indiscreet. I cannot suppose that such an indiscretion was authorized?[38]

It is to these early exchanges that the fierce partisanship that broke out years later between the supporters of Liszt and Wagner can be traced. By 1872, the year in which Wagner laid the foundation stone of the Bayreuth opera house, this question of who was influencing whom was on many lips. The ardent Wagnerian Heinrich Esser, the conductor of the Vienna Court Opera, spoke for many when he wrote: "What will happen when [Wagner] is dead and can give us no more new works? Then will his imitators, the long-haired Lisztians, descend upon us en masse, and ruin, by their exaggerations, everything that the master has built up by a lifetime of work."[39]

37. NZfM, issues of June 17, June 24, August 5, and August 19, 1859.

38. Letter of October 7, 1859. WBB, pp. 125–26.

39. Letter from Heinrich Esser, the conductor of the Vienna Court Opera, to the publisher Schott, dated 1872. See IRW.

With the passing years the battle lines hardened further. By the time of the first Bayreuth Festival, in 1876, the divisions ran deep among many of the delegates. Wagner was by now perceived by the world in a very different light from the composer he had been twenty years earlier. He had become an artist of international renown; he no longer needed Liszt, and Liszt's supporters were quick to observe the ingratitude of a man whose name and fame had been kept alive by their hero during the dark days of a Swiss exile with a price on his head. Long forgotten, too, were the performances of Wagner's music put on in Weimar, often at Liszt's personal expense, at a time when the exile's music was banned from the rest of Germany. Ten years later still, we find the Schmalhausen diary, dealing as it does with the painful events of July 1886, fairly seething with contempt for Wagner, his family, and his cohorts. It is easy to see in Schmalhausen's indictment of the Wagners merely the opinion of a confused young woman. Yet she was simply expressing views that were not uncommon among Liszt's circle of friends and pupils, although, needless to add, they were not the views of Liszt himself.

VIII

There is a revealing coda to this story that bears retelling. After it had become clear to Carl Alexander that Weimar was not to have the honor of receiving Liszt's remains, he took the first steps toward honoring Liszt's memory through the creation of a *Stiftung* whose primary task was to initiate a number of projects to ensure that Liszt's memory was kept alive. The Hofgärtnerei, which had been the composer's home in Weimar since 1869, and was already known the world over as the site of his famous masterclasses, was turned into a permanent Liszt Museum. This building already housed some of his most valuable possessions, and after the death of Princess Carolyne, her daughter Princess Marie Hohenlohe very generously donated the large sum of 70,000 gulden toward the foundation, together with much Liszt memorabilia that had belonged to her mother. This priceless collection included musical manuscripts, letters and diaries, gold medals and diplomas, and lithographs and paintings, together with many valuable objects acquired by Liszt during his golden years as a touring virtuoso—the silver breakfast service presented to him in 1840 by the Philharmonic Society of London, a jade-and-gold clock from his admirers in St. Petersburg in 1842, a bejewelled casket given to him by the Grand Duchess Maria Pawlowna, and finally his Bechstein grand piano and the small Ibach upright on which he used to accompany his students.[40]

The museum was opened on May 22, 1887, and a hundred or more visitors filled the rooms and spilled out onto the garden outside. They included members of Weimar's royal family; Princess Marie Hohenlohe and her husband Prince Konstantin; and many friends, disciples, and pupils. Profes-

---

40. By far the most comprehensive catalog of the original holdings of the Liszt Museum is the one issued by Adolf Mirus, in 1892, that is five years after the exhibition was opened (see MLMW).

sor Adolf Stern from Dresden delivered the inaugural address. The visitors then wandered through the rooms marveling at the extraordinary retrospective exhibition covering more than sixty years of Liszt's life. Not a single member of the Wagner family turned up. May 22 happened to be Richard Wagner's birthday, and nothing was to be allowed to disturb this hallowed day, especially a celebration that reminded everyone that Liszt had his own place in the history of music which had nothing to do with Wagner. Was this choice of date a deliberate provocation? By itself it amounts to nothing. Neither does the publication of Wagner's *Mein Leben* in 1911, Liszt's centenary year. But taken together with everything else we have observed, the timing is difficult to dismiss. Cosima visited the Liszthaus only once, later in 1887, in the company of her daughter Eva. They were given a private tour by Liszt's old housekeeper Pauline Apel, who had been appointed the official in-house custodian.[41] As Cosima stared at all the precious objects that memorialized some of the major triumphs of Liszt's remarkable career, she turned to Eva and remarked in French (so as not to be understood by Frau Apel): "All these beautiful things are lying around here doing no good. I would like to know why my fa-

41. Pauline occupied this position until her death in 1926, while Dr. Carl Gille was the first curator. After Gille's own death in 1899 this increasingly important position was taken over in turn by Karl Müller-Hartung, who served 1899–1902, Aloys Obrist, who served 1902–10, and Peter Raabe, who served 1910–44. It was during the long tenure of Raabe that the *Stiftung* brought to completion the first collected edition of Liszt's music in thirty-six volumes, under the distinguished editorship of Busoni, Bartók, Vianna da Motta, d'Albert, and Raabe himself, among others.

ther didn't leave them to his family."[42] The comment suggests that Cosima had no idea of the real meaning of her father's life. A better purpose, from Cosima's point of view, might have been to melt down the medals and use the proceeds to pay off the debts of the Wagner festival.

In fact, the festival of 1886 had suffered a serious deficit, and at the time Cosima visited the Liszt museum it was weighing heavily on her mind. People had not turned out in the large numbers that she had hoped for. Some performances, especially the matinées, had attracted audiences of fewer than three hundred people, and Cosima had been obliged to paper the hall. Her landmark production of *Tristan,* the first ever mounted in Bayreuth, was hardly the runaway success she had expected. People in general were sceptical of Cosima's ability to direct the festival; the Germans expected a catastrophe and stayed away in droves, although enough foreign visitors attended to maintain the semblance of an international event. According to Moulin Eckart, things were no better in 1887, and for one performance of *Tristan* only twelve tickets were sold, and the house had to be papered in its entirety.[43] It was not until the 1888 production of *Parsifal* that Bayreuth was able to staunch the flow of red ink. In brief, the Wagner festival was in a fragile state, its future uncertain. Cosima's remark about her father's material legacy, crass as it was, stemmed from the current impoverishment of the festival,[44] from her

42. "Liszt's Pauline." Cuk, *Neue Wiener Journal,* September 26, 1926.

43. MCW, vol. 2, p. 118.

44 Adolf von Gross had great worries about the entire festival. There was

anguish about its future, and with it, the future of Richard Wagner.

IX

This, then, was the background of turmoil, dissension, and resentment against which the Schmalhausen diary was written and against which it has to be read, otherwise it cannot take on its full significance. It is an important fragment in a psychological jigsaw puzzle, now well over a century old; and once that fragment has been fitted into place, the picture that emerges is fuller and more sharply defined than ever before. The relationship between Liszt and Wagner was a human drama, filled with outcries and asides, ranging from the extremes of loving friendship on the one hand to acts of hostility and ungovernable anger on the other. Small wonder that so much of the information that helps us to plot this complicated relationship was censored, suppressed, or sealed: Wagner's *Mein Leben,* Liszt's will, Cosima's diaries, and finally Schmalhausen's account of Liszt's last days all fall into one or another of these categories. Biographers and historians alike rarely have to contend with such revealing documents, and this one is likely to change the balance of their

---

no reserve fund. He tells us that in 1886, as the lamentable state of the box office became clear, he and his colleagues sent out urgent letters and telegrams to friends and colleagues taking the waters in the nearby Bohemian spas, urging them to visit the festival. For further information on Bayreuth's finances, and especially the deficit of 1886, see PA, p. 98.

work. To anyone reading at the time of Liszt's death the Schmalhausen narrative it would have appeared to be incomprehensible. But now, 125 years later, as we hear this 22-year-old woman give voice to her innermost feelings, it is as if she is addressing us from beyond the grave. And we understand her message. From across the great divide she provides us with yet new insights into a topic that continues to fascinate us all.

Requiescat in pace

Sources

AMZ   *Allgemeine Musik-Zeitung.* Cited by issue.

BBM   Bache, Constance. *Brother Musicians: Reminiscences of Edward and Walter Bache.* London, 1901.

BFL   Burger, Ernst. *Franz Liszt: Eine Lebenschronik in Bildern und Dokumenten.* Munich, 1986.

BWL   *Briefwechsel zwischen Wagner und Liszt.* 2 vols. Leipzig, 1887.

CBL-G   Carthe, Erich. "Ein Beitrag zur Liszt-Gedenkfeier." *Liszt Saeculum* 59 (1997): pp. 20–21. Reprinted from a German newspaper of 1911, probably a verbatim report from Lina Schmalhausen herself.

CLBA   Csapó, Wilhelm von, ed. *Franz Liszts Briefe an Baron Antal Augusz, 1846–78.* Budapest, 1911.

CLC   Carl Lachmund Collection. Special Collections Department of the Performing Arts Division of the New York Public Library. Call no. JPB 92-1.

DMML   Damrosch, Walter. *My Musical Life.* New York, 1923.

EFLE   Eckhardt, Mária. *Franz Liszt's Estate.* 2 vols. Budapest, 1986–93.

FLL   Friedheim, Arthur. *Life and Liszt: The Recollections of a Concert Pianist.* Edited by Theodore L. Bullock. New York, 1961.

GL   Göllerich, August. *Franz Liszt*. Berlin, 1908.

GFLW   Gottschalg, Alexander. *Franz Liszt in Weimar und seine
            letzten Lebensjahre*. Berlin, 1910.

GLB   Goddard, Scott, ed. and trans. *Letters of Hans von Bülow
            to Richard Wagner and Others*. New York, 1931.

GLK   Göllerich, August. *Franz Liszts Klavierunterricht von
            1884–1886: Dargestellt an den Tagebuchaufzeichnungen
            von August Göllerich, von Wilhelm Jerger*. Regensburg,
            1975. (Translated, edited, and enlarged by Richard
            Louis Zimdars as *The Piano Masterclasses of Franz Liszt,
            1884-1886: Diary Notes of August Göllerich*. Bloomington
            and Indianapolis, 1996.)

GSA   Goethe- und Schiller-Archiv, Weimar. Liszt Collection
            held by the Nationale Forschungs- und Gedenkstätten
            der klassischen deutschen Literatur in Weimar.

IRW   Istel, Edgar. *Richard Wagner im Lichte eines zeitgenössischen
            Briefwechels*. Die Musik, Heft 15/16, pp. 1370–71. Berlin,
            1902.

KFL   Kapp, Julius. *Franz Liszt*. Berlin, 1909. Rev. ed., Berlin,
            1924.

KLMR   Keeling, Geraldine. "Liszt and Mason & Risch." In *New
            Light on Liszt and His Music: Essays in honor of Alan
            Walker's 65th Birthday*, edited by James Deaville and
            Michael Saffle, pp. 75–90. Stuyvesant, 1997.

KWL   Kloss, Erich, ed. *Briefwechsel zwischen Wagner und Liszt*.
            2 vols. Leipzig, 1910.

LCS   Litzman, Berthold. *Clara Schumann: Ein Künstlerleben*.
            3 vols. Leipzig, 1902–08.

LDML   La Mara. *Durch Musik und Leben im Dienste des Ideals*. 2
            vols. Leipzig, 1917.

LL   *Living with Liszt: The Diary of Carl Lachmund, an*

Index

Page numbers in italics refer to main annotations.